*The Brave New World of the Enlightenment*

*Ann Arbor*
*The University of Michigan Press*

# THE BRAVE NEW WORLD OF THE ENLIGHTEN-MENT

**by LOUIS I. BREDVOLD**

Designed by Stuart Ross
Copyright © by The University of Michigan 1961
All rights reserved
Published in the United States of America by
The University of Michigan Press and simultaneously
in Toronto, Canada, by Ambassador Books Limited
Library of Congress Catalog Card No. 61-10987
Manufactured in the United States of America
by Vail-Ballou Press, Inc., Binghamton, N. Y.

 *ACKNOWLEDGMENTS*

These six lectures were originally given at St. Olaf College, Northfield, Minnesota, on the Louis W. and Maud Hill Foundation, in October and November 1958. They have been revised and somewhat expanded for publication. In the first lecture I have used, with the permission of the editor, some passages from my article on "The Meaning of the Concept of Right Reason in the Natural Law Tradition," which appeared in the *University of Detroit Law Journal* in December 1958. Stanford University Press has also granted permission to use excerpts in my second lecture from my article on "The Invention of the Ethical Calculus" in their volume, *The Seventeenth Century, From Bacon to Pope,* issued in 1951 in honor of Professor Richard Foster Jones. In preparing these lectures for the press I have constantly recalled the six happy weeks of my association with the faculty and students of St. Olaf.

*Louis I. Bredvold*

# CONTENTS

# CONTRACTS

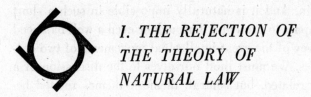

# I. THE REJECTION OF THE THEORY OF NATURAL LAW

The purpose of these discourses is to examine some of the ideas of the Enlightenment that have had a continuing importance in the thought of the modern world. Such a statement of purpose probably seems, in our present state of mind, to promise only one more ceremony of praise and gratitude for the seventeenth and eighteenth centuries. The very designation of a period as one of enlightenment implies, of course, that we rejoice over the great intellectual progress achieved at that time and congratulate ourselves on inheriting all its manifold benefits. We recall that Europe then turned scientific and stopped burning witches. Everybody accepted the fact that the earth is round and revolves around the sun, and not the sun around the earth. The nature of electricity was discovered. Great advances were made also in the practical arts and sciences, and the steam engine was invented. In political thought people became more rational and democratic. The critical spirit was permitted free play in religion and philosophy as never before. In a word, the Enlightenment was the period when Europe really emerged from the Middle Ages and the Modern Mind was born.

It is not my purpose, however, to repeat this familiar

strain. And it is naturally impossible in such a short compass to present a thorough or even a well-balanced survey of the great intellectual movements of two centuries. We must limit ourselves to the discussion of a few related, but central, themes—themes related because they are all concerned with the important urge of man to understand himself and his condition on this planet. We shall find that some modern ideas, currently regarded as of recent origin, were widely accepted two or three centuries ago. It may be worth while to study them in their historical setting, in their early appearances, and in that context to reassess them and inquire into their truth and their value. There is an advantage for critical thought in this psychological distance. We can more calmly observe these familiar ideas as they operated in the past, far from our own heated controversies. We are in a better position to judge and evaluate them as we observe what thinkers did with them in a distant time, and what they did with thinkers. At any rate, it is with this general purpose, and in this critical spirit, that I wish to direct your attention to some ideas of men and society in the Enlightenment.

It is surely a commonplace that new ideas often make old ideas seem valueless, or at least out-of-date. The history of a great intellectual change, such as the Enlightenment, must record the significant abandonment of the old as well as the acceptance of the new. First, I propose to speak primarily about an old idea which was thought in the Enlightenment to have become obsolete. I believe that this approach to our general theme will quickly get us to the heart of the whole matter.

It has been observed many times by many people that words of common use are far more complex than scientific terms, and far more difficult of definition. They trouble the lexicographer far more than the technical terminology devised by scientists. They also trouble the philosopher, and even the layman when he is unavoidably faced with philosophical problems. Two such words, both crucial in philosophical and ethical thinking, are *law* and *nature*. Both have in common usage more than one meaning, and indeed meanings that are mutually contradictory. Even philosophers have down through the centuries been confused by them. They have been important words in the history of our Western civilization for more than two thousand years—important in speculative thought and equally important for their bearing on the vital issues in our practical conduct of life.

Before we look at their history, let us scrutinize for a moment some of the various meanings of these two words with which we are all familiar. By Nature we commonly mean such phenomena as are studied in the sciences, or, more broadly, phenomena which actually exist. But then we also speak of the nature of a living thing to designate its potentiality, not what it actually is, but what it might become under certain conditions. And we have art, which in one breath we contrast with nature and in the next declare to be an

idealization of nature, what the French have called
*la belle nature,* the achievement of a perfection not to
be discovered in actuality. In moral thought we practice the same kind of duality. We repeat the old adage
of the Stoics that man should live according to Nature.
We understand them to have meant, of course, not that
the moral man is one guided by the laws of physics and
chemistry, but by laws of an entirely different order,
by his higher nature, the fidelity to which might on
occasion require even the disregard of the laws of natural science. In our daily speech and in our actions we
acknowledge the fact of the double nature of man. As
human beings we must perforce live in two worlds,
one, the world that actually exists, the other, the world
that ought to be and often is not. Both worlds we call
Nature.

As there are two kinds of Nature, there must also
be two kinds of laws of Nature. There are the natural
laws of the sciences, which have this peculiarity that
they are never broken and do not need effort by us to
sustain them. No convention needs to assemble with
speeches and committee reports on how to strengthen
and enforce the law of gravitation. But the other kind
of law of Nature, the moral law, poses for us, indi-
vidually and collectively, the problem, not only how
we may be righteous ourselves—a heavy enough responsibility—but also how we may make righteousness
prevail. There is one law for man and one for thing,
said the sage Emerson. As we are both man and thing,

we have both laws to deal with. The great secret is to distinguish between them. They are qualitatively different; they require us to operate simultaneously on two different levels of experience. We have different ways of learning about them, different ways of understanding how they are true. We must not apply to the one the tests which are applicable only to the other. The laws of physical nature are never broken; what seems to be an exception turns out to be only the discovery of one more law. By this process of investigation our knowledge of the laws of the physical world is continually expanded and improved. But we cannot proceed in this way with moral laws. When a moral law is broken we discover, not a new law, but only one more sinner. Moral laws are being broken, have always been broken, and presumably always will be broken by us human beings, miserable as we are. It is the condition of our humanity under which we groan. When Moses descended from the mountain with the two tables of the Law, he beheld below on the plain his people dancing around a golden calf which they had fashioned to be their god. Already the first commandment was broken, even as it was being promulgated. When Moses broke the stone tablets against the rock, he gave us a symbol of the fractures of the laws themselves which men have been guilty of in all ages all over the world. But the breaking of the tablets did not nullify the Law, and the infractions of the moral law likewise do not invalidate it. On the contrary, the more numerous and

the more flagrant the violations, the more resolutely
human nature asserts and affirms the principle of the
law.

Out of this dichotomy in man there developed the
great historic tradition of the Law of Nature as a legal
and moral concept, the concept with which we are now
to be concerned. Its origins are lost in the mists of
antiquity. We find Heraclitus of Ephesus about five
hundred years before Christ saying that the sight of
injustices among men taught them that there must be
such a reality as justice, eternal and immutable, and
that there must therefore be a "divine logos" by which
"all human laws are nourished." [1] It is worth while to
pause a moment and observe precisely what the process
was as this early philosopher described it. We note
that he does *not* say that certain indolent men of speculative temperament sit and dream about a divine logos,
a rational principle of an imaginary world above us,
and then look at the actual world about them and declare it imperfect. The process, as Heraclitus described
it, moves in the opposite direction, from the actual to
the ideal. Men saw injustices, they were disturbed, they
had to pass judgment on these practices. But as they
passed judgment they were inevitably invoking a law.
Where is this law, and what is its nature? It may or
may not be written on the tables, it may or may not as
yet have been decreed by authority. But when men
recognized injustice and judged it as such, they *thereby*
committed themselves to the idea of justice; call it
what you will, call it the moral law, the conscience of

mankind, the sense of decency, the Law of Nature, we cannot escape it without reducing human beings to mere things. The law for man is different from the law for thing; we live in a world of standards and values; every day we live is a day of judgment.

About all we can say, then, about the origin of the doctrine of the Law of Nature is that it sprang out of the constitution of human nature. How it developed in early Greek thought is obscure, but Aristotle in his lectures on rhetoric in the fourth century before Christ informed his young students that the Law of Nature was good enough and common enough as accepted legal doctrine to be useful in pleading cases at law. He even illustrates and fortifies his statement by quoting the speech of Antigone in the play by Sophocles in which this heroine appeals to an eternal law, higher than any edict of the state:

> Not of to-day nor yesterday
> Is this the law, but ever hath it life,
> And no man knoweth whence it came or how.[2]

This doctrine of the Law of Nature, which emerged so obscurely in Greek thought, passed, primarily through the influence of Cicero, into Roman philosophy and legal thought and thence into the main stream of Western civilization. For nearly two thousand years it was one of the controlling principles of juristic philosophy and international law. Its history has been studied by many learned scholars and a bibliography of the subject would alone run into a volume. But we are fortunately not so much concerned with the details of the history of the doctrine as with its essential nature and importance, its importance for the past, for our time, for any time. And one of the best and most persuasive interpreters of it was none other than Cicero.

His treatise on the principles of law, *De Legibus*, is really a charming informal dialogue between himself, his friend Atticus, and his brother Quintus.[3] Cicero is enjoying a holiday from his busy life of law and politics in the capital city. On his country estate at Arpinum he converses leisurely with his friends under the famous Marian oak or on the banks of the river Liris. They press him to use his "odds and ends of time" to write a treatise on the civil laws of Rome. But Cicero rejects the idea of producing only another handbook for practicing lawyers. "To what task are you urging me?" he replies. "Do you want me to write a treatise on the law of eaves-troughs and house walls? Or to compose formulas for contracts and court documents?" No, said Atticus, write on the laws of the ideal state: "For I note that this was done by your beloved Plato, whom you admire, revere above all others, and love above all others."

Cicero is thus drawn into an immediate discussion of the nature of law as a philosophical concept, digesting into his exposition the doctrines of the Stoics and the spirit of his beloved Plato. He will not discuss the laws regarding eaves troughs or the liability due to rickety walls, but will try to set forth the source of law, the right principles of law, and its proper value and function in the life of mankind. In such a discussion, he says, the civil law will be confined to a small and narrow corner. The subject must be treated broadly; in searching into it we must bring out clearly "what Nature's gifts to man are, what a wealth of excellent possessions the human mind enjoys, what the purpose is to strive after and to accomplish which we have been born and placed in this world, what it is that unites men, and what natural fellowship there is among them. It is only after all these things have been made clear," says Cicero, "that the origin of Law and Justice can be discovered."

Let us try to reduce his informal utterances to a system. First of all, we can gather what he thinks is a mistaken conception of law. The science of law cannot be based merely on a digest of the edicts of praetors or other government authorities. It cannot be learned, Cicero remarks, "from the many pestilential statutes which nations put in force. These no more deserve to be called laws than the rules a band of robbers might pass in their assembly." Nor can we found the principles of Justice on "the decrees of peoples, the edicts of princes, or the decisions of judges," lest we find ourselves committed to agreeing that "justice would sanction robbery and adultery and forgery of wills, in case these acts were approved by the votes or decrees of the populace." Votes and decrees cannot change the Laws of Nature nor make the bad into good. Clearly, Cicero is not satisfied with the theory that law is in the last analysis only a command issued by powerful authority. That, he says, is the vulgar crowd's definition of law. As we shall see in a moment, it is just this vulgar crowd's definition of law that has dominated juristic thought in the nineteenth and twentieth centuries, since the Enlightenment.

On the positive side, what Cicero insists on is a conception of law such as would make it irreconcilable, not merely with political anarchy, but also with moral anarchy. We must be granted that it is legitimate to inquire whether the justice being actually administered is just. We must therefore search for the origin of law and justice, he says, not in the opinions of men, nor in the will of those in position to command, but in Nature. This Nature can be known by the reason of man when it is full grown and so perfected that it can rightly be called wisdom. Cicero is not here referring to the discursive reason or the reason of scientific method, but to an immediate and intuitive apprehension of moral and spiritual values. This is, indeed, the divine element in man. For reason, Cicero insists, is the first common possession of man and God. "But those who have reason in common, must also have right reason in common. And since right reason is Law, we must believe that men have Law also in common with the gods. Further, those who share Law must also share Justice: and those who share these are to be regarded as members of the same commonwealth. If indeed they obey the same authorities and powers, this is true in a far greater degree; but as a matter of fact they do obey this celestial system, the divine mind, and the God of transcendent power. Hence," concludes Cicero, "we must now conceive of this whole universe as one commonwealth of which both gods and men are members."

Obviously, this is a Nature not to be discovered by physical science. It is a moral universe, different from the physical universe, and one in which, as Cicero repeatedly emphasizes, all men have common citizenship and all men are equal. The Law of Nature must therefore be conceived of as existing before any written law and as continuing to exist in spite of the actuality of bad laws and inequitable decrees, because it is Right Reason, understandable by man, but existing in the divine mind as the source of law and justice.

All this may not sound much like the conversation of a lawyer in our Christian land, but it impressed the lawyers of the Roman Empire, who adopted Cicero's little treatise as a classic. The doctrine of the Law of Nature made its way among the jurists of the Empire, and almost six hundred years after Cicero it was written into the preamble of the Justinian Code. It was taken over by the early Church Fathers and St. Augustine, and in the Middle Ages the great mind of Thomas Aquinas organized the previous ideas about it into an impressive system which dominated speculation on the subject for centuries. Among the many later treatises bearing on it, it must suffice to mention *The Laws of Ecclesiastical Polity* by the English divine Richard Hooker, published in 1594, and the great treatise on international law published by the Dutch scholar Grotius in 1625. The Law of Nature was not regarded as an abstruse or esoteric doctrine by the general public of the Renaissance. What we call "international law" they called "the Law of Nature and of Nations," and that phrase was sufficiently understandable to the average man for Shakespeare to incorporate it several times in the dialogue of his plays. When a contemporary of Shakespeare, the great lawyer Sir Edward Coke, declared that "Reason is the life of the law; nay, the common law is itself nothing but reason," he was in effect claiming that the Law of Nature was the guiding spirit of the English Common Law. Our more modern world is also far more indebted to this ancient doctrine than it would like to acknowledge. When we say that certain Rights are Natural, we are speaking the language of Cicero and Hooker, not of anthropology. To look more specifically to our American heritage, we have the proposition which we have just found also in Cicero, that all men are created equal. This proposition may be examined as a scientific statement by the discursive reason; but if understood strictly on this level, it can obviously not be proved true, whether considered as psychology or sociology or anthropology or physiology. The proposition can appear to be true only as it is apprehended by the intuitive reason, and in that sense, as the Declaration of Independence says, it is self-evident, and scientific demonstration is irrelevant. As we reflect on this and other similiar principles basic to our American ideals and our philosophy of law, we can realize that as a people we are really deeply committed to the Right Reason of the tradition of Natural Law.[4]

However, in the eighteenth century we come into a climate of opinion in many ways unfavorable to the doctrine of the Law of Nature. In this climate the venerable plant of the centuries seemed to be dying, and was indeed by many people thought as good as dead. New intellectual interests, new modes of thinking, new doctrines, took the place of the old. The Law of Nature was subjected to a continuous destructive criticism by a succession of great and influential writers all over Europe. Attacks on the Law of Nature are, indeed, just about as ancient as the doctrine itself. But from the sixteenth to the eighteenth century these attacks were gaining in frequency, prestige, and influence. They were a part of the great revolution of human thought which we call the Enlightenment. By the year 1800 the Law of Nature had come to be generally dismissed as a relic of medievalism or worse, and its rejection as a distinguishing mark of an emancipated modern mind.

The tone and manner of these attacks may be well illustrated already in Montaigne, who of all the great writers of the sixteenth century was regarded as the most modern and congenial to the enlightened readers of the following two centuries. For generations his *Essays* were the favorite reading of the educated and half-educated people of Europe. He was one of the most successful popularizers of all time. His scathing

strictures on the Law of Nature will probably sound
quite familiar to us, even as we read them in the antiquated English of Florio's translation. There is, first,
the sceptical objection that there does not seem to be
any agreement among men as to what these Laws of
Nature are, nor even how many there are.

What goodness is that [Montaigne asked scornfully]
which but yesterday I saw in credit and esteem, and to-
morrow to have lost all reputation, and that the crossing of
a river is made a crime? What truth is that, which these
mountains bound, and is a lie in the world beyond? But they
are pleasant, when to allow the Laws some certainty, they
say that there be some firm, perpetual and immovable, which
they call Natural, and by the condition of their proper essence are imprinted in mankind: of which some make three
in number, some four, some more, some less: an evident
token that it is a mark as doubtful as the rest.

This was the sceptical dialectic of ancient Pyrrho-
nism, which Montaigne learned from the writings of
Sextus Empiricus. By it he was emancipated, not only
from the doctrine of the Law of Nature, but from all
belief in any universal moral truth ascertainable by
reason. What then is morality? It is nothing, he an-
swered, but custom:

The laws of conscience which we say to proceed from
nature, rise and proceed of custom: every man holding in
special regard, and in inward veneration the opinions approved, and customs received about him, cannot without remorse leave them, nor without applause apply himself unto
them.

Any investigation into the source or origin of our sacred laws must be disillusioning, and even dangerous:

Laws take their authority from possession and custom [he argued]. It is dangerous to reduce them to their beginning: In rolling on, they swell, and grow greater and greater, as do our rivers: Follow them upward unto their source, and you will find them but a bubble of water, scarce to be discerned, which is gliding so proud, and gathers so much Strength.[5]

These are arguments with a modern ring. People who do not know any other Latin can tell us that the word "moral" is derived from *mores,* meaning "custom."

But for a really striking modern analogue to Montaigne we can go to learned authority, to Justice Oliver Wendell Holmes, who was fond of making merry with the doctrine of the Law of Nature. Writing in the *Harvard Law Review* in 1918 he said:

What we love and revere most is generally determined by early associations. I love granite rocks and barberry bushes, no doubt because with them were my earliest joys that reach back through the past eternity of my life. . . . The jurists who believe in natural law seem to me to be in that naive state of mind that accepts what has been familiar and accepted by them and their neighbors as something that must be accepted by all men everywhere.

Thus Justice Holmes, like Montaigne three centuries earlier, dissipated the ethical imperative into mere custom. With all proper respect to the memory of the great Justice, we cannot allow that he here shows himself either a sound moral philosopher or a competent introspective psychologist. He surely misunderstood his own nature. There is a profound difference between the enjoyment of granite in a landscape and the approbation we bestow on granite in the human character. The two states of mind have quite different relations to the constitution of human nature. The Justice is generally reported to have had granite in his character, and we may be sure that he would have had an adequate reply to any counsel before the Court who would have had the temerity to suggest that the nine men in black gowns were so many bundles of inherited custom and prejudice.

But heckling is the popular dialectic of the modern world, and it has been the favorite procedure of those who wanted to dispose of the Law of Nature as a principle of jurisprudence. The question then arises, if the Law of Nature is eliminated, what principle takes its place? Law must have authority, and there is little authority in mere custom. There is only one alternative, power or might. As the German language has it, we must choose between *Recht* and *Macht*. If law does not have in itself an inherent imperative, such as we can recognize and willingly subject ourselves to, then law will have to secure our submission by force. Of course, all government must have might; we are all of the opinion that we are overtaxed, but we pay our taxes because we have to. However, if we insist on a complete severance between law and ethics, if we deny that there is any higher law to which both king and subject must bow, then we bestow upon whatever kings there are an absolute power; in a democracy we must accept as inescapable a jungle warfare of politics in which various factions and interests play a complicated game in an effort to control the law for their own selfish purposes. Such developments could be abundantly illustrated from ancient and modern history. But are such ideas seriously advanced as legal theory? The answer is that they are, and by very respectable authority; they are modern ideas. Brooks Adams was a scion of the noble stock of the Adams family of Massachusetts, though it might be thought that he, like his brother Henry Adams, represents it in a late and deteriorated stage. In 1906 he published a volume with the title, *Civilization and the Law*. Here are some representative passages:

The rules of the law are established by the self-interest of the dominant class, so far as it can impose its will upon those who are weaker. . . . There are no abstract legal principles, any more than there is an abstract animal apart from individual animals. . . . The law is the resultant of the conflict of forces which arises from the struggle for existence among men. Ultimately these forces become fused under the necessity of obtaining expression through a single mouthpiece, and that fusion, effected under pressure, we call the will of the sovereign. . . . The dominant class, whether it be priests or usurers or soldiers or bankers, will shape the law to favor themselves, and that code will most nearly approach the ideal of justice of each particular age which most perfectly favors the dominant class. . . . Law is not the command of a sovereign, assuming the Sovereign to be

a power apart from the subject community. Law is the resultant of social forces, and the Sovereign is the vent through
which this resultant expresses itself.[6]

It is entirely possible that this description by Adams
has in it a good deal of sociological fact, although one
might question whether sociology has as yet shown that
the struggle ends quite so automatically in fusion. Curiously, Adams sounds very much like an indignant
satirist. But were he a satirist, he would have been con-
trasting what is with what should be and thus have implied a standard of justice; he would have demanded
that men of honor and principle should step in and
restore order. But Adams was writing scientific sociology, not satire; he was not a reformer or a Hebrew
prophet, but a thorough and unflinching disciple of
that scientific movement of the nineteenth century rep-
resented by Auguste Comte, who called his philosophical sociology Positivism. And we are concerned here,
not with the question whether there is an element of
truth in the description of actual society which Adams
presented, but with quite another question: what can
scientific positivism do for us in the way of giving us
a satisfactory theory of law, and, by implication, of
ethics and human nature? What Adams gives us is a
depressing view, sour enough to satisfy the hereditary
taste of the Adams family, but unfortunately plunging
us into a theoretical fatalism which unbraces our moral
muscle and, indeed, constitutes a negation of the great
moral force and energy of Brooks Adams's own an-
cestors.

Scientific positivism cannot escape from the consequences of its own theory and its own method. Since it limits itself strictly to a description of what actually is, it cannot transgress beyond that into the sphere of what ought to be; therefore it has to deny itself not only satire, which is a form of criticism, but any and all conceptions of ideal law and ethics. As applied to government, the theory inevitably leads to the conclusion that the government which has the power *de facto* is the source of law, that law is nothing but the commands of those who have the power, that there is no other test or criterion by which we can pass judgment on a law as good or bad, that we may indeed rise in revolt against authority if we feel injured and have sufficient resources, but that to condemn it morally is unscientific, and to ask whether our justice is just is simply unreal and futile.

As is often the case with modern ideas, the Positivism of the nineteenth century was an old philosophy with modern refinements. We can equally well study its dilemma in juristic theory by examining the ideas of Thomas Hobbes, who in the seventeenth century developed a comprehensive scientific philosophy of human nature, of morals, and of society and government. Hobbes was a heretic; like a good modern, he was proud to discard the ideas of the Ancients and begin all things anew. "There is no such *summum bonum* [or greatest good]," he said, "as is spoken of in the books of the old Moral Philosophers." Moral laws cannot be universal, for there is nothing universal but names. But

Hobbes was sure that one thing all men desired, and that was peace and quiet. However, all men are also selfish, so completely selfish that any unselfish motive or act is psychologically impossible. As he built up his system Hobbes therefore arrived at the conclusion that the only way peace could be secured on earth was by a government so strong that it could force all the selfish subjects into a harmonious submission.

Thus he became the philosopher of political absolutism. Law he defined as nothing but command, not the command of any man to any man, but of such authority as has sufficient coercive power over the subject, who is in turn bound by the institution of government to obey. Laws thus become the measure of justice and injustice, not justice the measure of the law. Nor is law something on which men can exercise their reason; for, as he explains, law is law simply because it is the will of the sovereign power. He argues that any member of a society is presumed to have given over all his rights to the sovereign power of government, that the subject has therefore given *carte blanche* approval in advance to anything government might do, and consequently "that nothing the sovereign power can do to a subject, on what pretence soever, can properly be called injustice or injury." With inscrutable nonchalance Hobbes illustrates this new twist which he gives to the old maxim that the king can do no wrong. He brings up the case of David, who, after seducing Bathsheba, sent her husband Uriah to the hottest battle front, where he was killed. This action, Hobbes explains, "was not

an injury to Uriah; but to God. Not to Uriah, because the right to do what [the King] pleased was given him by Uriah himself: and yet to God, because David was God's subject, and prohibited all iniquity by the Law of Nature." This reference to the Law of Nature is a useless concession, an insulting irony; so quick-witted a man as Hobbes must have been aware that he was making the principle of justice not only extralegal, but extraterrestrial as well, and therefore offering no deliverance to any oppressed person in the whole muddled world. He does not allow either law or justice to be amenable to any discussion by reason. Law is pure and simple command.[7]

Well, Hobbes had his day of glory, and it is long since passed. But plausible ideas do not die with their champions, but reappear with new vigor when the climate becomes favorable to them. And a theory of law and sovereignty, essentially as Hobbes formulated it, was advanced by the scientific jurisprudence of the nineteenth century. A highly respected and influential exponent of it was John Austin, whose lectures between 1830 and 1860 at the universities of London and Oxford went into many editions and enjoyed the standing of a classic. Austin defined law as "a rule laid down for the guidance of an intelligent being by an intelligent being having power over him." By the qualification of intelligence he did not, however, admit anything like the right reason of the Natural Law tradition; he explained that he only meant to exclude animals from the sphere of law. He held that the only test of the

validity of a law is whether the sovereign has the power
to enforce it by inflicting evil or pain.[8] Like Hobbes,
Austin thus erased any distinction between *de jure* and
*de facto;* both severed law from morality or justice,
and both accepted the only conclusion left to them, of
basing law on force. In the settled and quiet age of
Victorian England such a theory advanced by a lec-
turer at Oxford did not arouse any public commotion.
Those interested in the subject accepted it as one more
step forward in modern intellectual progress.

What happened was that in the nineteenth century
international law as well as all other departments of
legal theory became scientific and positivistic. Down
into the eighteenth century the Law of Nature had been
accepted by all European nations as the foundation of
international law. One has only to look into the great
authoritative treatises of Grotius, Puffendorf, and
Wolff. No written covenant with signatures affixed was
then considered necessary to outlaw such atrocities in
war as poisoning wells or shooting a soldier approaching with a white flag. But in the nineteenth century this
unscientific doctrine could no longer be honored, and a
new principle was adopted that international law is
only what is contained in signed treaties and covenants,
and binding only on those who have signed. When most
of the nations were involved in World War II and a
mass of treaties consequently voided, a professor of
political science threw up his hands in despair: "There
is no longer any international law. I am a professor of
international law, and I have no subject matter." And

when the war was over and the trials for war crimes began, unforeseen difficulties appeared. The Nuremberg Tribunal, for instance, proceeded on the principles of positive law; that is, that there can be no conviction for a crime if there is no statute binding on the accused and defining the crime and decreeing the punishment for it. There are legal authorities who argue that the Court was able to surmount this difficulty only by tacitly admitting the applicability of Natural Law principles, stating that these trials were a "question of justice." It was going beyond the principles of scientific jurisprudence to say, as the Court did: "So far from it being unjust to punish him, it would be unjust if his wrong were allowed to go unpunished." [9]

But it is not necessary to accumulate numbers of such situations in which it has been found expedient to appeal beyond the limitations of a scientific jurisprudence to the authority of the Law of Nature, or, if the expression is preferred, to the conscience of mankind. Reference has been made earlier to the popularity in our era of the doctrine of Natural Rights. In this realm of thought the whole modern world on this side of the Iron Curtain seems in agreement, and the whole modern world thus unwittingly pays its homage to Natural Law. For the doctrine of Natural Rights is, both historically and logically, a derivation from the more comprehensive principle of Natural Law. Strangely enough, the modern public does not seem to see the connection, even though the word *Natural* assumes exactly the same preconception in both phrases.

There are tens of thousands who shout confidently about their Natural Rights for one who has given even a thought to Natural Law. This contraction of the principle of Law into Rights is a misfortune of modern thought which must be blamed on the Enlightenment. It was John Locke, more than any other one man, who prepared the modern world for the idea that Natural Rights could stand independent, and self-sustaining.

By this severance of Rights from Law he provided the central doctrine of revolutionary thought for the eighteenth century and down to our time. Viscount Bryce remarked, somewhat inaccurately, that the doctrine "which had been for nearly two thousand years a harmless maxim, almost a commonplace of morality, was thus converted into a mass of dynamite which shattered an ancient monarchy and shook the European continent." [10] Bryce surely minimized unduly the Law of Nature in describing it as a harmless commonplace of morality, but he was obviously correct about the explosive force of the doctrine of Natural Rights. Whenever it is pressed hard and unqualified by the idea of Law, the doctrine of Rights leads to revolution, disruption, and excessive individualism. Everybody wants his rights and everybody is ready to secede to get them. One of the reasons for the precarious state of Western civilization at the present moment, for its lack of cohesiveness, is the universal insistence on rights without a balancing emphasis on obligations. But rights do not exist, morally or legally, except under laws; otherwise the demand for rights, whether sacred or not, becomes an uncontrollable centrifugal and anarchic force.

However, the doctrine of Natural Rights has the merit that it once more reunites law and morality. Its present popularity may eventually lead our age to a more sympathetic and understanding interest in Natural Law. When the corollary proposition is received with such general approbation, there should be a hearing for the theorem from which it is derived. There is, indeed, some substantial ground for such a hope. Since late in the nineteenth century there has been a significant reaction in juristic thought against positivistic jurisprudence and a greater reliance on Natural Law, not only in this country but in Europe. The Fourth Hague Convention of 1907 stated explicitly in its Preamble that the "laws of humanity" and the "dictates of the public conscience" are part of international law. Roscoe Pound, dean of the Harvard Law School, observed in the *Harvard Law Review* in 1911 that "it is not an accident that something very like a resurrection of natural law is going on the world over." One has only to look into our current law reviews and into the new scholarly works on jurisprudence coming every year from the press, to appreciate that the question of the nature of law is really agitating our own time. It must be a basic problem, because, unless we understand it rightly, we cannot understand ourselves or the constitution of human nature. We are so made that in a society of human beings we must have both Might and Right operating; but we must decide which is the

superior principle; there is no third alternative. This
is not an academic problem that can be left to the de-
liberations of specialists in political science; it is the
concern of all humanity. Shakespeare, a shrewd observer of human nature, put in the mouth of the saga-
cious Ulysses, in *Troilus and Cressida*, a prediction as
to what would happen to mankind if "force should be
right":

> then right and wrong
> Should lose their names, and so should justice too.
> Then everything includes itself in power,
> Power into will, will into appetite,
> And appetite, a universal wolf,
> So doubly seconded with will and power,
> Must make perforce a universal prey,
> And last eat up itself.

For a generation we have been threatened with this
very danger.

In the Middle Ages one of the subjects for dispute
in the schools was whether it is *jus quia jussum* or *jus
quia justum*, is it law because it is commanded or because it is right. This is not such an empty quibble on
words as it may seem. For if we believe that law is law
merely because it is enforced upon us, we can be obe-
dient but we can never feel within ourselves any moral
allegiance to it. The man who never obeys a law for
any other reason than his fear of the penalty is not
really a good citizen, even though he may be shrewd
enough to remain all his life peaceable; Cicero says of
such a man that he is merely thick-skinned. Of course,

all of us obey the laws, whether we think them good or bad, because we want to avoid the penalties. But we must have something more than this, some better motive for observing the law, if we are to have a good society. We can be citizens of a truly good society only as we recognize that the law, however faulty, is the attempt of man to establish justice; that it is the attempt to make operative in human society those universal principles of right which can be apprehended by Right Reason. The approbation and homage which we give to the law when we recognize it as justice, this, said Cicero in antiquity, unites all men everywhere in a common citizenship—this, said Edmund Burke in modern times, is the one sure and strong ligament of human society.

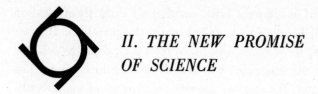

## II. THE NEW PROMISE
## OF SCIENCE

The seventeenth century inaugurated a new epoch in
the history of the human mind by its many brilliant
discoveries in mathematics and science. The greatest
of them all, the one which most profoundly influenced
all the habits of thought of the modern world, was the
discovery that all motion can be measured mathematically. This discovery was achieved step by step by a
succession of scientists and mathematicians over a
period of nearly one hundred years. We need not follow in detail its complicated history; we must restrict
ourselves to some salient features of it. The problem
that disturbed the scientists of the time was, at least to
begin with, primarily astronomical, raised by the new
Copernican astronomy and made more acute by the
careful observations of the orbits of the planets around
the sun. It had been believed from time immemorial
that these orbits were perfect circles, and that as the
symbols of the divine perfection of the Creator they
could not conceivably be anything but circular. But
now the observations of the astronomers revealed that
they were in fact elliptical, and that the universe was
therefore irrational and lawless. It was a profound
shock to astronomers as well as to other people to learn
that the heavenly bodies were rambling about in such

an irregular and unpredictable a manner. The lament of John Donne in 1611 is well known:

> And new philosophy calls all in doubt,
> The element of fire is quite put out;
> The sun is lost, and th' earth, and no mans wit
> Can well direct him where to look for it. . . .
> 'Tis all in pieces, all coherence gone;
> All just supply, and all relation.[1]

The new idea of the earth as a planet revolving around the sun produced no such dismay as the scientific demonstration which seemed to reduce the world to chaos and disorder.

But even as Donne was writing, science was already beginning to advance toward the true principle of order. Galileo was studying the swinging of the chandelier in the cathedral of Pisa and dropping weights from the leaning tower. He found that both motions were measurable, that mathematical formulas were applicable to both. This revelation may be considered to mark the beginning of the new philosophy of motion. But mathematics did not as yet have the means for reducing planetary orbits to measurement. This deficiency was soon made good, however, as two or three generations of enthusiastic mathematicians all over Europe developed this study with amazing rapidity, and among many other discoveries learned how to apply mathematics to any kind of curve. Finally, Sir Isaac Newton tested all this knowledge by computing the orbit of the moon around the earth; he resolved it into two simple motions, a forward motion of the moon of a certain velocity, and a second motion of the moon falling toward the earth by force of gravitation. By computing these two motions and their modification of one another, Newton demonstrated that the orbit of the moon can be stated in terms of mathematics and that it can be predicted as far into the future as one might wish to compute. The same methods were naturally applicable to the orbits of planets around the sun. Order was thus restored to the universe; and this order was not something speculative, not a matter of faith, but computed and demonstrated by mathematics.

When Newton published his masterpiece, *Philosophiae Naturalis Principia Mathematica*, in 1687, he placed the keystone in the great arch of mathematical astronomy and physics. Natural philosophy had arrived at the absolute certainty of mathematics. As the total of such a measurable nature must ever be constant quantitatively, Newton advanced the necessary corollary of the conservation of matter and energy, that is, that in the whole universe there is never any loss of either matter or energy. As human beings are also part of this mechanism, Newton provided modern materialistic philosophy with a fresh orientation in mathematical physics.

Newton himself, however, did not draw any materialistic deductions from his science; he was a religious man as well as a cautious scientist, and he stopped short of philosophy. But long before he gave the world his triumphant demonstration, even while he was still in the cradle, other philosophers, less cautious, jumped

to the conclusion that the new philosophy of motion
was as good as demonstrated already and that it should
be applicable not only to physics and astronomy but
also to man and society. Among the most notable of
these was Thomas Hobbes.

Thomas Hobbes (1588–1679) became a philosopher by sheer chance. Up to the age of forty he was just
another Oxford graduate, earning his living as a tutor
and traveling companion to the sons of an aristocratic
family. He had never studied mathematics at Oxford;
but at the age of forty he picked up a copy of Euclid's
*Geometry* and read it through with a sense of a great
revelation; here was the first and only book he had ever
found in which every proposition was absolutely in-
controvertible. Why were there no other books like it?
And why not write a philosophy of man and society,
that troublesome subject of controversy in all past ages,
in a similar style of step by step demonstration? This
project Hobbes decided to make his own. About this
time he also learned about Galileo's study of motions,
and his basic equipment was complete. By analyzing
the psychology of man in terms of motion and setting
forth his exposition as nearly as possible in the manner
of geometrical reasoning, he elaborated in a long series of books what he confidently believed was a defin-
itive and conclusive solution to the problem of the nature of man and society. Hobbes spiced his style with
wit and irony, and sometimes with that supercilious-
ness which is so becoming in a modern speaking of his
predecessors. Geometry, he said, "is the only science

that it hath pleased God hitherto to bestow on mankind." [2] For the want of this method all previous philosophy had been absurd, whereas by means of this
method all moral and political problems could have
been solved long ago and peace have been established
on earth. In the Epistle Dedicatory to *De cive* he
strikes this modern note:

> Truly the Geometricians have very admirably performed
> their part. . . . If the moral philosophers had as happily
> discharged their duty, I know not what could have been
> added by human industry to the completion of that happi-
> ness, which is consistent with human life. For were the na-
> ture of human actions as distinctly known as the nature of
> quantity in geometrical figures, the strength of avarice and
> ambition, which is sustained by the erroneous opinions of
> the vulgar, as touching the nature of right and wrong, would
> presently faint and languish; and mankind should enjoy
> such an immortal peace, that (unless it were for habitation,
> on supposition that the earth should grow too narrow for
> her inhabitants) there would hardly be left any pretence for
> war. [3]

Hobbes was one of the first to promise a scientific
Utopia in which vices would "faint and languish."

When we examine this new philosophy which prom-
ised peace on earth and the disappearance of vice, we
find only a crude form of scientific materialism ter-
minating in a most rigorous political absolutism. Man
is an animal, very much like a machine, with passions,
appetites, and desires which can never be anything but
selfish and which therefore can be controlled only by
a government strong enough to coerce all subjects to

absolute obedience. As we have already observed,
Hobbes defined law as simply command enforced by
penalty. He formulated a political philosophy of absolutism more uncompromising than that of any other
philosopher. It cannot be said that he exerted any practical influence on any government in his time or later.
But some aspects of his thought fascinated the French
*philosophes* of the eighteenth century. And he should
probably be given the credit of being the first notable
writer to proclaim that we could solve our social and
moral problems if we only made our social sciences
as scientific as mathematics and physics.

But this was an idea which occurred quite naturally
to others also in the seventeenth century, when the mar-
velous new developments in mathematics flushed men
with all sorts of Utopian hopes. Hobbes had a contemporary co-worker in France in Descartes, with whom
he was slightly acquainted. But the two men differed
greatly in abilities, aims, and methods. Descartes was
a profound mathematician, whereas Hobbes was little
more than an amateur; Hobbes was trying to square
the circle while Descartes was discovering analytical
geometry. But Descartes labored on the elaboration of
what he called a "universal mathematical science,"
a vast a priori system which should begin like geometry with incontestable maxims and deduce from them
a comprehensive philosophy of the world and man.
"All Philosophy," he said, "is like a tree, of which
Metaphysics is the root, Physics the trunk, and all the
other sciences the branches that grow out of this trunk,

which are reduced to three principal, namely, Medicine, Mechanics, and Ethics. By the science of Morals, I understand the highest and most perfect which, presupposing an entire knowledge of the other sciences, is the last degree of wisdom." [4] Ethics would thus be, not only as certain a science as physics, but a development out of the principles of mechanics and physics. He confessed to Mersenne in 1630 that he was not making the progress he hoped for on an a priori medicine, "based on infallible demonstration," a medicine so absolutely certain that it would achieve conquest over sickness, the infirmities of old age, and perhaps even over death itself. Unfortunately, the system had not yet been developed to the point of efficacy when death overtook Descartes. But he assured his friend Chanut in 1646 that ethics was easier to demonstrate with certainty than medicine, though he had spent more time on the latter. His study of physics, he said, had greatly helped him reach incontestable fundamental principles in ethics.[5] But he accomplished nothing substantial on this vast project; his universal mathematical science was still only a dream and a hope when he died.

However, he bequeathed to his successors his method of constructing ethics as a deductive and infallible science, perhaps itself mathematical in nature, but at least proceeding by a kind of reasoning analogous to that of mathematics. When Spinoza died in 1677 he left in manuscript his great ethical treatise with the title *Ethica more geometrico demonstrata*. The *more geometrico* became quite the fashion in treatises on ethics and law in the late seventeenth century, even as late as Christian Wolff's treatise on legal theory, published at Halle in 1749, with the title *Jus Gentium methodo scientifica pertractum.* Through Leibnitz we discover the now forgotten professor at the University of Jena, Erhard Weigel (1625–99), who was in his day a notable figure, enjoying a high reputation even beyond the narrow world of learning. Among his many publications was an *Ethica Euclidea,* mentioned by Leibnitz in a letter in 1663. If we may judge his speculations from his *Idea Matheseos Universae* (1669), the only work of his available for inspection, he held that the basic principles of all knowledge are to be discovered in a science which he called *Panto-metria,* to which moral philosophy and jurisprudence as well as metaphysics must be subordinated. This *Pantometria* is of course the universal mathematical science of which Descartes dreamed. Leibnitz was a student at Jena in 1663, and he recalled many years later that Weigel had been ingenious in inventing diagrams to represent moral aspects and relations, but Leibnitz judged these unsatisfactory as "serving the memory in the retention and arrangement of ideas rather than the judgment in the acquisition of demonstrative knowledge." [6] Though Leibnitz was also haunted by the dream of a general or universal science, he was great enough to see the inadequacies of Descartes and the futility of some of the efforts of Weigel.

The earliest attempts of Leibnitz were directed toward the solution of political questions by the geometrical method. In 1669, when he was twenty-five years old, he tried to settle by this method the selection of a new king for Poland. He published at Danzig a little book, *Specimen demonstrationum politicarum pro eligendo rege Polonarum*, presenting his argument in the geometrical style of sixty propositions, accompanied by corollaries, and thus demonstrating that three candidates should be excluded and the fourth elected. Two years later, when he was in Paris on a diplomatic mission, he tried a second "Specimen of Political Demonstration" on Louis XIV, in which the geometrical method indicated that the French monarch should dispatch his armies from the Low Countries to Egypt to break the power of the Turk.

These were, however, youthful efforts, and Leibnitz soon undertook a more ambitious project, closer allied to the calculus than to geometry, and in method suggestive of the development of modern symbolic logic. He was far too subtle to be satisfied with such crude statements as that of Hobbes, that reasoning is merely a kind of arithmetic using the processes of addition and subtraction. What he sought to achieve was the Cartesian idea of a universal mathematical science, but he also understood from the beginning that the logic and mathematics available to Descartes were inadequate for this purpose. Before 1680 he began work on an encyclopedic treatise, of which only plans and fragments remain. The resemblance of his plan to that of Descartes is obvious. He believed that he could discover a "general science" (*scientia generalis*) which would include not only geometry (in a transcendent form) and mechanics (based on geometry), but also a *"logique civile"* or *"logique de la vie,"* which would provide a calculation of probabilities applicable to all practical questions and in particular to legal problems. For this purpose he devised a sort of symbolic mathematical logic which he called *"la charactéristique universelle,"* by which he hoped to reduce all reasoning to a combination of signs, to a calculation. In a letter written about 1690 to the Duke of Hanover he expressed his confidence in this project. This new characteristic (a new way of thinking as well as of writing) he called *"le juge des controverses,"* and he regarded it as an infallible method of settling disputes. "If controversies were to arise," he said, "there would be no more need of disputation between two philosophers than between two accountants. For it would suffice for them to take their pencils in their hands, to sit down to their slates, and to say to each other (with a friend to witness, if they liked), 'Let us calculate.' " [7] If Leibnitz could only have completed this system, it would have settled for us all our moral, social, and political problems, giving us such foresight, as a French scholar has put it, as though we had been present and overheard all the secrets of God at the creation of the world.[8]

As this *furor mathematicus* continued unabated into the eighteenth century it is not surprising that Pope mentions it in his *Dunciad*. Pope was no mathematician, but it seems likely that he had something more than circle-squarers in mind when Dulness triumphs over Science, Wit, and Logic, but "Mad *Mathesis* alone was unconfined." When religious Mystery is described as expiring in Mathematics, the allusion may possibly be to that ardent theologian *more geometrico*, Samuel Clarke, as well as to the Deists. However, the only mathematician to be honored by name in either the text or notes of *The Dunciad* was a certain Scottish divine John Craig, who in 1699 published a curious book with the title *Theologiae Christianae Principia Mathematica*. Craig worked out a calculus of moral evidence and its decay with the passage of time; his figures showed that in 1699 the evidence in favor of the truth of the Gospel was equivalent to the testimony of twenty-eight contemporary disciples, but that it would diminish to zero in the year 3144.[9] The celebrated Gilbert Burnet, Bishop of Salisbury, was sufficiently impressed with this learning to find a living for the Reverend Mr. Craig in his own diocese.

A more distinguished victim of this *furor mathematicus* was Francis Hutcheson, who in 1725 published an important treatise, *An Inquiry into the Original of Our Ideas of Beauty and Virtue*, and later became an influential professor of moral philosophy at Glasgow. He announced on the title page that his work was also an attempt to "introduce a mathematical calculation in subjects of morality." This able and eminent man filled pages of his book with a strange and futile pretence at algebraic reasoning. Some quotation is necessary to do justice to this attempt:

To find a *universal Canon* to compute the *Morality* of any Actions, with all their Circumstances, when we *judge* of the Actions done by our selves, or by others, we must observe the following *Propositions,* or *Axioms.*

1. The *moral Importance* of any *Agent,* or the *Quantity of publick Good* produc'd by him, is in a *compound Ratio* of his *Benevolence* and *Abilitys:* or (by substituting the initial Letters for the Words), $M = B \times A$.

2. In like manner, the *Moment* of *private Good,* or *Interest* produc'd by any Person to himself, is in a *compound Ratio* of his *Self-Love,* and *Abilitys:* or (substituting the initial Letters) $I = S \times A$.

3. When in comparing the *Virtue* of two Actions, the *Abilitys* of the *Agents* are equal: the *Moment* of *publick Good* produc'd by them in like Circumstances, is as the *Benevolence:* or $M = B \times I$.

And so on until Hutcheson reaches the conclusions that $BA = M - SA = M - I$ and $M = B - S \times A = BA - SA$.[10] It is hardly necessary to observe that these capital letters are mere abbreviations, not algebraic symbols, and that any attempt to subject them to algebraic manipulation is absurd. Laurence Sterne was prompted to comment that Hutcheson "plus's and minus's you to heaven or hell, by algebraic equations —so that none but an expert mathematician can ever be able to settle his accounts with S. Peter—and perhaps S. Matthew, who had been an officer in the customs, must be called in to audit them." [11]

Such efforts as these, considered merely in themselves as philosophical projects, were no doubt unimportant failures. But considered as expressions of a new temper of mind, of a new conception of the universe, and of a new approach to the problems of humanity, they are both important and revealing. The scientific spirit was beginning to permeate the mind of Europe, and the average intelligent person was ready to believe that a new era of unprecedented human felicity was just beginning. Fontenelle, for fifty years the Perpetual Secretary of the French Academy of Sciences and perhaps the greatest popularizer of science in any day, wrote about the turn of the century that the spirit of geometry had already exercised a good influence on the intelligence of the general public, even on those who were not instructed in that study. Books on all subjects, he said, were being written with more order, more precision, more logic.[12] But more was involved in the new modern spirit than the mere clarity of style welcomed by Fontenelle. Geometrical reasoning is deductive, and there was of course nothing new about deductive reasoning as such. Nor was there anything new in the observation that geometry could begin with a few exact definitions and deduce from them a whole volume of exact demonstration. The novelty of the "modern" geometrical spirit was the application of the same method to writing whole volumes of exact demonstration of the science of human nature. The belief that an irrefutable geometry of morals and politics was about to be written was the first article in the new creed. As it was commonly expressed at that time, what the world awaited was the Newton of the science of ethics and human society.

In view of the prestige and authority which John Locke enjoyed among the later *philosophes* in France, it is noteworthy that in his *Essay Concerning Human Understanding* he repeatedly affirmed his conviction that morality is as capable of exact demonstration as mathematics.[13] He was well aware of the importance in such geometrical reasoning of choosing correctly (one cannot suppose wisely, for there is no wisdom in geometrical reasoning), and defining precisely, a set of basic concepts. In discussing "trifling propositions" he dealt severely with that circularity of reasoning which is the pitfall in deductions from definitions.[14] He heaped scorn on the proof offered by Descartes that the soul is a thinking substance: "It is but defining the soul to be 'a substance that thinks,' and the business is done. . . . No definitions that I know, no suppositions of any sect, are of force enough to destroy constant experience."[15] Thus spoke Locke the empiricist. But when he tried to present ethical propositions as certain as those of mathematics he reasoned as follows:

The *relations* of other *modes* may certainly be perceived, as well as those of number and extension: and I cannot see why they should not also be capable of demonstration, if due methods were thought on to examine or pursue their agreement or disagreement. 'Where there is no property there is no injustice,' is a proposition as certain as any demonstration in Euclid: for the idea of property being a right to anything, and the idea to which the name of 'injustice' is given being the invasion or violation of that right, it is evident that these ideas, being thus established, and these names annexed to them, I can as certainly know this proposition to be true, as that a triangle has three angles equal to two right ones.[16]

The proposition itself comes merely to this that there can be no invasion of property rights where there is no property, a proposition as certain as geometry but hardly worth printing in a book. And as for defying common sense and "constant experience," there could be no more unacceptable definition of justice than one which would limit its application to the law of property; it would leave the case of Uriah as desperate as under the absolutism of Hobbes—unless both Bathsheba and Uriah's life were defined as property. Curiously, a comment on Locke by the youthful Berkeley almost echoes Locke's derision of Descartes: "To demonstrate morality it seemed one need only make a dictionary of words, and see which included which. . . . Locke's instances of demonstration in morality are, according to his own rule, trifling propositions." [17]

After 1700, however, we find a significant shift in the methods and aims of these scientific students of morals and society. Less interest was taken in the great mathematical systems dreamed of by Descartes and Leibnitz. But the geometrical method of reasoning, it was discovered, could be combined with an observation of the real phenomena of the world. A scientific investigation into the psychology of the individual and the behavior of man in society could form the basis for generalizations or simple laws from which a whole series of valuable truths might be generated, *more geometrico.* The philosophers of the eighteenth century thus managed to bring into a union the empiricism of Bacon, whose memory they venerated, and the confidence in deduction of Descartes, from whom they inherited an unshakeable faith in the efficacy of reason. In this spirit they produced a whole series of treatises on morals, society, and government, all of which were based on the premise that now, at last, emancipated science could solve all the perplexing problems of man. Now, at last, it was understood that man, like physical nature, must be subject to ascertainable natural laws, and therefore equally manageable by a controlling reason. All the age-old problems of man were to be solved by the new science of man.

The formulators of this new science were not all in agreement on all points; far from it. For moral geometry, unhappily, seemed always to fall short of the scientific ideal of universality; each treatise had its own peculiarities reflecting the individual interests of the author; the moral geometry of France and England also reflected the differences between the two countries in popular moral attitudes, political traditions and experience, and even in religion. Such individual and national differences are of course disconcerting when they appear in a mathematical science. But all of these speculators, in France and England, also had a great deal in common, so that it is possible to formulate their main doctrines into a system. Hartley, Priestley, and Godwin in England, Condillac, Baron d'Holbach, Helvetius, and Condorcet in France, all began their theories with the same premises, developed them in the same spirit and with the same method, and arrived at quite similar conclusions.

After first assuming that human nature must be considered merely as an extension of physical nature and equally subject to the law of cause and effect, they began with the psychology of John Locke. He had elaborated the old philosophical adage that we have nothing in our minds that has not come to us through our senses, touch, taste, sight, smell, and hearing. The content of our minds is built up out of these sensations. How Locke explained the combination of these sensations into larger and more complex ideas and general notions of reasoning, such as we have to use when we read Locke, we cannot stop to consider. There may be some difficulties concealed in his account. But one important conclusion drawn by Locke and maintained strenuously by him is that we do not have any so-called innate ideas, or ideas that are inherent in the structure of the mind. The human mind is at birth a *tabula rasa*, a clean slate for experience to write on. But if that is the whole truth, then as we grow up we become what our experience, our education, our environment, combine to make us. Our slates are written full as we live. Locke did not draw this conclusion himself; he would probably have been shocked could he have known what his followers in the next hundred years did with it in his name. But they saw the great opportunity which did not occur to Locke. They saw that if a man at a given time can be explained in terms of his experience, and completely explained in this way, he is after all a passive creature; in our day we could compare him to a mechanical brain; feed into the machine certain data, and out will come with the inevitability of scientific law the conclusions which follow from the data. Locke had not allowed himself to believe that man is a machine; but his followers did not allow themselves to believe anything else. This mechanistic conception of human nature was the favorite starting point for the revolutionary moral and social speculation of the eighteenth century.

In France La Mettrie published in 1749 a book with the self-explanatory title, *Man a Machine.* Between 1746 and 1780 Condillac produced a succession of psychological works on the same theme. Condillac is best known in our time for his famous illustration of the nature of man. Imagine, he said, a statue in marble or bronze just completed by the sculptor. Imagine that the sculptor is so delighted with this resemblance to a real man that he wishes to make a real man out of it. Imagine that he is able to bestow upon this statue the powers of sensation, touch, smell, taste, sight, and hearing, one after the other. When the statue has thus acquired all the five senses of man, behold, it is a man, completely equipped to acquire also the experience necessary to lead the life of a human being. Such was the constitution of human nature, simple, machine-like, operating under the laws of cause and effect, on the basis of which the French *philosophes* elaborated their social science.

In England we have David Hartley and his famous
book, *Observations on Man,* also published in 1749,
the same year with La Mettrie's book in France. Hartley was a Cambridge graduate, a religious man, who
had been prevented by some scruples from becoming
a clergyman and had therefore turned physician. He
did not scoff at religion as did his contemporaries in
France. His work enjoyed a considerable prestige and
influence for half a century. Coleridge named his son
after him, and Wordsworth in his youth believed that
the explanation of the power of great poetry in general,
and certainly of his own in particular, could be found
in Hartley's theory of the association of ideas. But
Hartley believed as firmly as the French atheists in
the mechanistic explanation of man. Man, he said, is
made up of vibrating particles, which he called "vi-
bratiuncles," and everything that happens within man
is governed by the law of necessity. As he put it, "the
cause of the cause is also the cause of the thing caused,"
and therefore it is inconceivable that there could be
any missing link in the chain of causes and effects
which make up the cosmic process. Our sensations are
the effects within us of the stimuli from the world out-
side us, and are combined inexorably by various laws
of association. It was this law of association that Hartley hoped would do for the science of human nature
what Newton had done for physics and astronomy.
Where, then, can there be a place for religion? Hartley
found a place; God is the first cause, and therefore the
cause of all; we are all tied to God by the chain of ne-

cessity. We need not follow the implications of such a theory further; but before leaving Hartley we may note that he expressed a hope that in the future all such enquiries as his could be stated in mathematical form and that all psychological and moral terms reduced to concepts of pure quantity.

From these premises what kind of moral and social science could possibly be developed? The philosophers thought the best, because the most demonstrable and certain, and therefore also the most desirable and useful. They were writing for an age of reform and revolution, they made themselves the spokesmen for the current agitation for a better world. They could offer the assurance that all efforts, whether of reform, revolution, or reconstruction, could now proceed on a sure scientific basis. All the psychological discussions of the *philosophes* were preambles to their programs for the improvement of morals, society, and government.

This was the argument elaborated by Helvetius in his celebrated and notorious treatise, *De l'esprit,* published in 1758. Helvetius was of German ancestry, but his grandfather settled as a physician in Paris and his father followed the same profession, becoming one of the physicians to the Queen. From his father Helvetius inherited a fortune, but even better, a position at the French Court which brought him a lucrative government contract as farmer-general of revenues. In 1751, at the age of thirty-six, he gave up this post and retired to a life of wealthy leisure to write his treatise on the mind of man. In his country house and his mansion in town he entertained the advanced thinkers of Paris and distinguished visitors from all over Europe with fine dinners, at which the conversation was usually both witty and philosophical. Horace Walpole told in one of his letters of the rumor that Helvetius was on the point of coming to England with his two beautiful daughters and fifty thousand pounds apiece with the intention of bestowing them on two English aristocrats if he could find any that were virtuous. The jibe was intended to be a home-thrust, for Helvetius was a philosopher dedicated to the study of virtue.

To be sound and fruitful this study must of course be mathematical. Like Hobbes and Locke and all other geometricians of morals, Helvetius must begin with right definitions. For "if words were precisely defined, and their definitions ranged in a dictionary, all the propositions of morality, politics, and metaphysics would become as susceptible of demonstration as the truths of geometry." [18] Like the other French *philosophes* he accepted as axiomatic Locke's theory of the mind as produced by sensations, and like them he also turned this theory into the first principle of materialism and mechanism. Like Hobbes, he argued that this mechanical human being can act only from self-regarding motives. More specifically, Helvetius explained that all appetites and desires can form impulses in man only because their satisfaction gives us pleasure and their frustration gives us pain. This pleasure-pain theory, which is so familiar to students of later English

Utilitarian philosophy, he proposed as the substitute for the old traditional moral values. Moreover, all pleasure and pain must be a form of "corporeal sensibility." And "from the moment we regard corporeal sensibility as the first principle of morality, its maxims cease to be contradictory; its axioms all linked together will bear the most rigorous demonstration; in short, its principles being freed from the darkness of speculative philosophy, will become evident, and the more generally adopted as the people will be the more clearly convinced of the interest they have to be virtuous." [19]

The doctrine that man always acts from self-interest, which Mme du Deffand said had been a secret every man kept locked up in his own breast until Helvetius published it to the world, seemed to Helvetius to be of the greatest service in constructing sound theories of society, education, and government. Society must be an arrangement by which all these selfish individuals learn to live together. This can be achieved only by education, which is the art of inspiring and managing the passions and desires of men. But education is not a mere matter of schooling; it is coextensive with life, and especially a matter of government. Indeed, legislation is not merely a part of education, but legislation and morality are one and the same science. As the basic principle of both education and legislation is the doctrine of self-interest, the whole problem of the lawmaker is quite simply to educate and control this motive. This should offer no difficulty; let us not be dis-

mayed by the publication of the whole world's secret;
we have the moral law of gravitation which offers us at
last the means of perfecting ourselves and our society.
From the statement of these clear truths Helvetius deduced "the perfectibility of the human mind or understanding." [20] From their operation he deduced the perfectibility of society. As he said:

> Being once assured that man always acts in conformity
> to his interests, the legislature may assign so many punish-
> ments to vice, and so many rewards to virtue, that every
> individual will find it in his interest to be virtuous . . .
> Make good laws; they alone will naturally direct the people
> in the pursuit of the public advantage, by following the
> irresistible propensity they have to their private advantage.
> . . . It is of little consequence that men be vicious; it is
> enough that they be intelligent. . . . Laws will do all.[21]

These naive speculations of Helvetius thus lead us at
last to an enlightened despotism with an enlightened
bureaucracy as the last best hope of mankind. We must
await the work of the lawmaker who will take over our
education as well as our laws, and who will so perfect
society that in seeking always our own enlightened
selfish interests we shall also achieve, without pain and
even without moral effort on our part, the beautifully
harmonized well-being of all society.

Unfortunately, officialdom in Paris did not set to
work on this plan. Instead they condemned the book
and burned a copy of it on the grand staircase of the
Palais de Justice; the lawyers also condemned it, and
so did the professors of the Sorbonne. However, all

this disapproval by the public authorities did not matter much; they were in the habit of burning books. The
treatise by Helvetius could still be bought surrepti-
tiously in France, and translations of it appeared all
over Europe. Helvetius became a European luminary.
What is of greater importance is that Helvetius of-
fended his friends, the members of his own philosophical circle, who were themselves also trying to be the
Newtons of moral science, and who were working on
some of the same assumptions as Helvetius. He
wounded them with his central doctrine of the essential
selfishness of human nature. Rousseau called the book
detestable, and Diderot took exception to many of its
general principles. These men were committed to a
more generous view of human nature; they believed, in
contradiction to Helvetius, in the unselfishness of man,
and even more than that, they believed that man is
naturally good and that it is from this principle that
all morals and legislation must begin. Helvetius repre-
sented but one aspect of the revolutionary thought of
his time. The other and seemingly contradictory trend
must be examined before we can understand the full
force of the storm that was to come.

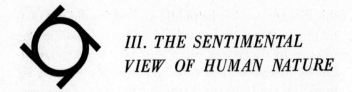

## III. THE SENTIMENTAL VIEW OF HUMAN NATURE

When Diderot and Rousseau and the other advanced thinkers of Paris denounced Helvetius for his contention that man is by nature selfish and cannot be anything else, it was not a mere clash of personalities. Two large historical movements met in contention. It will be helpful to cast a glance backward at their earlier developments from the seventeenth century on.

First of all we meet our old friend Thomas Hobbes; for we have already seen that he deduced from the new philosophy of motion that man is also a creature of motions, and that all his impulses must be self-regarding and directed either to securing pleasure or avoiding pain. Life is therefore a continual self-assertion, a desire for power and glory; a man must be engaged in ceaseless rivalry with his fellows. In this rivalry, to quote Hobbes, "to endeavour, is appetite. To be remiss, is sensuality. To consider our rivals behind us, is glory. To consider them ahead of us is humility. To lose ground with looking back, vain glory. To turn back, repentance. To be in breath, hope. To resolve to break through a stop foreseen, is courage. To break through a sudden stop, anger. To fall on a sudden, is disposition to weep. To see another fall, is disposition to laugh. To hold fast by another is to love. Continually to be out-gone is misery. Continually to out-go the other person is felicity. And to forsake the course, is to die." [1] Thus ends the creed. We may well agree with Hobbes that if this is the sum of human life, men can be governed only by an absolutely despotic state.

But what does Hobbes have to say about the ethical life, about ideas of right and wrong? Has he forgotten about morals and their place in human life? He has not forgotten about the virtues; in one place or another he discusses most of them. He does not use the words *right* and *wrong,* preferring *good* and *evil.* And "good and evil," he said, "are names that signify our appetites and aversions, which in different tempers, customs, and doctrines are different. When a man deliberates whether to do a thing or not, he does nothing else but consider whether it be better for himself to do it or not." [2] When Hobbes takes up the psychology of the individual virtues, he explains them as forms of selfish desires, disguised from most of us by an outward shell of pretence. When we think we are most unselfish, we are merely deluded; as a matter of fact the only possible motive for unselfishness must be the preservation of our feeling of contentment and comfort. Charity is the complacent exercise of power, in being able to assist others. Pity is imagination of future calamity to ourselves. He denied that we can have any disinterested love of goodness, even of the goodness of God, for, he observed, with that characteristic mixture of shrewdness and sarcasm of which he was a master, "the goodness which we apprehend in God is only his goodness to

us, as is evident from those many supplications we hear
every day made unto Him." It must be granted that
Hobbes was a sharp observer and a clever analyst of
human nature, and his witty cynicism appealed so
widely to the sophisticated and would-be sophisticated
people of his time that it alarmed sober men, both
church and lay.

But at the same time these sober men were alarmed
by the threat, both within the Anglican Church and
among Independent sects, of a spreading Calvinism,
which ever since the Reformation had had a considerable body of adherents in the Church of England. Calvinism meant, of course, a stringent doctrine of the
total depravity of man after the Fall, and when the Calvinists described the state of fallen man, with his mind
darkened and his will corrupted, the result offered
very little more hope than the philosophy of Hobbes.
It is illuminating in this connection to compare Hobbes
with a French contemporary, La Rochefoucauld, the
celebrated writer of cynical maxims. La Rochefoucauld
was a grand seigneur who, when the end of the Civil
Wars left him without military employment, went up to
Paris to enjoy the society of the metropolis. But there
he became an adherent of Jansenism, which was just
then rapidly gaining in strength even in very aristocratic circles. Jansenism may be briefly described as a
French Catholic parallel to Calvinism. Like Calvinism,
it pushed to their extreme form the Augustinian doctrines of the grace of God and the depravity of fallen
man. Under its influence Pascal became one of the

great religious writers. Racine was educated by the
Jansenists, and critics see a Jansenist influence in the
tortured souls of his tragedies, human beings suffering
anguish in their guilt, but completely helpless in the
toils of sin. The Jansenists were very expert in the application of their doctrines, in tracing out and exposing
the baseness and treachery of the human heart. It is
this view of human nature that is presented to us in the
witty and worldly *Maxims* of La Rochefoucauld. He
was no scientist and he did not have to state his observations as absolute universal laws. He qualified them with
such words as *often, ordinarily, sometimes,* and so on.
But for all that his method gives an impression of final-
ity. He expresses himself with more finesse than
Hobbes, but his method is exactly the same, and this
similarity is the more significant in that there is no
reason to think that either man ever heard of the work
of the other. Two different sets of ideas, one theological
and the other scientific, resulted in the same kind of
moral analysis of human nature. As we have seen,
Hobbes dissolved the so-called virtues into selfishness
in disguise. La Rochefoucauld dissolves the virtues
into disguised vices. Let us look at a few examples:

What men have called friendship is only a partnership,
a reciprocal arrangement of interests, and an exchange of
good offices; in short, it is only a business affair in which
self-love proposes to gain something.

In the majority of men gratitude is only a veiled desire
of receiving greater benefactions.

In the greater part of mankind love of justice is only
fear of suffering injustice.

Men would not live long in society if they were not dupes
of one another.

Reconciliation with our enemies is only a desire to better
our own condition, a weariness of strife, or a fear of some
unfortunate event.

Sincerity is ordinarily only a cunning deceit to secure
the confidence of others in us.[3]

The French Jansenist who wrote these observations
was obviously a well-bred man of the world. The Calvinistic divines of England were not so delicate in
their expressions; they thundered from the pulpit that
man is but a vessel of dung, a stink of corruption, and
by birth a child of the devil. The *Maxims,* published in
1665, immediately became popular in France and
among sophisticated readers in England. But in England the issue had already been joined; the down-
grading of human nature by Hobbes and by the Calvinists had converged on the same ethical problem. Consequently, men of moderation and sweet reasonableness
had already discovered that they had two different
enemies attacking them from opposite directions, and
they had to fight a battle on two fronts at the same time.

Under this pressure a considerable number of Anglican divines came to the defense of human nature.
They chose the middle way, quite in the tradition of the
Anglican Church, at least since Hooker. They rejected
the Calvinistic doctrine of total depravity, but they
were also careful not to go to the opposite extreme and
preach the heresy that man is capable of saving himself

by his own efforts, independent of the grace of God.
Their wrestling with this theological problem need not
concern us. We are interested in what they had to say
about human nature.

Among these Anglican apologists an honorable and
important place is held by a group of men appro-
priately called by historians the Cambridge Platonists.
We can set forth their conception of human nature,
which they admitted to be in a fallen and imperfect
state, by gathering some of their characteristic pro-
nouncements on the moral law.

Benjamin Whichcote (1609–83) declares in a sermon that the moral law is part of our constitution; it is
what he calls a truth of the "first inscription," implanted in man before any revelation. In his own
words, "it is connatural to man, it is the Light of God's
Creation, and it flows from the principles of which man
doth consist, in his very first Make: it is the soul's com-
plexion." This law therefore has "a deeper foundation,
greater ground for it, than that God gave the Law on
Mount Sinai; or that he did after engrave it on tablets
of stone; or that we find the Ten Commandments in the
Bible. For God made man to them, and did write them
upon the heart of man, before he did declare them upon
Mount Sinai, before he engraved them upon tablets of
stone, or before they were writ in our Bibles; God made
man to them, and wrought his Law upon men's hearts;
and, as it were, interwove it into the principles of our
reason; and the things thereof are the very sense of
Man's Soul, and the image of his mind, . . . The Law

externally given was to revive, awaken man, after his
apostasy into sin, and to call him to remembrance, ad-
vertency, and consideration. And, indeed, had there
not been a law written in the heart of man, a law out-
side him could be to no purpose." [4] Thus Whichcote
describes the moral law in terms almost identical with
those used by Cicero in his exposition of the Law of
Nature. Whichcote, of course, does not neglect to observe that the reason of man has become unreliable
and sluggish in the state of apostasy and sin, but Cicero had also granted that the reason of man, as we
find it, generally stands in need of much perfecting.
The whole sermon by Whichcote could be properly described as a Christianized version of the Law of Nature.

This philosophical affiliation of the Cambridge Platonists is equally striking in a treatise called *The Light
of Nature*, by Nathanael Culverwel (1618–51), published in 1652 and several times reprinted. The title
itself is a doctrinal commitment, and it is further defined by the motto or text, taken from the Book of
Proverbs (xx:27): "The understanding of a man is
the Candle of the Lord." Culverwel defends against
the Calvinists the use of reason in religion, a divine
gift. "Look but a while upon the parentage and original
of the Soul and of Reason, and you'll presently perceive that it was the Candle of the Lord." [5] Culverwel
devotes several chapters specifically to the Law of Nature and to a demonstration that the moral law is
founded in the natural and common light of Reason.

Like Whichcote, he insists that the moral law is inter-
woven with the nature of man; the Gentiles could discover it in their own natures as easily as the Jews in
theirs; like other expositors of the Law of Nature he
quotes Paul's Epistle to the Romans (ii:14–15): "For
when the Gentiles, which have not the law, do by nature the things contained in the law, these, having not
the law, are a law unto themselves; Which show the
work of the law written in their hearts, their conscience
also bearing witness, and their thoughts the mean while
accusing or else excusing one another." The Apostle
thus provided Scriptural authority for the doctrine of
the Law of Nature; but he also provided the basis for
an inference; for if the Law is written in the hearts of
the Gentiles and is operative in them, depraved and un-
illuminated as their minds must be, then fallen humanity has some good in it after all; in fact, it must
have a great deal of good in it. We must be something
more than just vessels of dung and sinks of iniquity if
we have written in our hearts the eternal law of Divine
Reason. As Whichcote had also counseled: "Reverence
God in thyself: for God is more in the mind of man
than in any part of the world besides; for we are made
after the image of God." [6] The personalities as well as
the doctrines of the Cambridge Platonists were gentle
and moderate. Few controversialists have been so sweet
and amiable.

But even the calm and reflective Culverwel could on
occasion raise his voice to an eloquent declamation
about so glorious a theme as the Law of Nature, present

in the hearts of all kinds of men all over the world.
"Look," he exclaims, "upon the diversities of Nations,
and there you will see a rough and barbarous Scythian,
a wild American, an unpolish'd Indian, a superstitious
Ægyptian, a subtle Æthiopian, a cunning Arabian, a
luxurious Persian, . . . an elegant Athenian, . . . a
desperate Italian, a fighting German, and many other
heaps of Nations, . . . and tell me, whether it must
not be some admirable and efficacious Truth, that shall
so overpower them all, as to pass current amongst them,
and be owned and acknowledged by them." And Culverwel will not permit his readers, just because they
are Christians and Englishmen, to affect a scornful and
superior attitude toward these barbarous, superstitious, cunning, desperate, fighting populations around
the world. "Have you weeds and briars and thorns in a
garden? No wonder then that you meet with more in a
wilderness. Do Christians blur and blot the Law of
Nature? No wonder then that an American [Indian]
seeks quite to rase it out." But Culverwel goes one step
further; he bears down on his civilized and Christianized English readers with a remark of the famous Salmasius. This learned man tells us, he says, "that he
had rather search for Nature's Law in a naked Indian
than in a spruce Athenian; in a rude American, rather
than in a gallant Roman; in a mere Pagan, rather than
in a Jew or Christian. . . . For those nations that have
more of art and improvement amongst them, have so
painted Nature's face, have hung so many jewels in
her ear, have put so many bracelets upon her hand,

they have clothed her in such soft and silken rayments as that you cannot guess at her so well as you might have done if she had nothing but her own simple and neglected beauty. . . . So that the learned Salmasius . . . chooses rather to fetch the Law of Nature from a Scythian, from a Barbarian; there he shall see it without any glosses, without any superstructures, without any carving and gilding." Of course, neither Culverwel nor Salmasius were especially interested in, or well informed about, the naked Indian, either of India or America. They were merely exploiting all the arguments they could find in support of the Law of Nature. But as they were arguing with all possible persuasiveness, they were drawn quite innocently into a eulogy of primitive man, into endorsing the concept of the Noble Savage, into an implied proposition that civilization has adversely affected morals.[7] Neither Culverwel nor Salmasius could have foreseen that in the next hundred years these same ideas, so seemingly innocuous, were to become driving forces in a great intellectual revolution of Western civilization.

These are the ironies in the history of ideas. Many a great man has had ardent disciples that he would have had to disown could he have lived long enough to know about them. Ideas are very slippery; they sometimes change their nature even as we handle them. A little overemphasis here, a little concession there, something new is added, and before we are aware of it our whole thinking is turned in a new direction. That is how the Cambridge Platonists became a part of an historical development leading ultimately to ideas quite alien to their real spirit.

Culverwel's eulogy of the Noble Savage had no direct influence on the history of that idea. It was already flourishing in the seventeenth century, and Culverwel merely borrowed it for an occasion. But the Cambridge Platonists as well as a number of other Anglican divines at that time were drawn by the common purpose of defending the goodness of human nature into alluring descriptions of the inward happiness of the good man. When we are good we are happy. We naturally feel a delight as our natures develop morally to flower and fruition. "Vice," said Whichcote, "is contrary to the nature of man, as man; for it is contrary to the order of reason, the peculiar and highest principle in man." Heaven itself, he said, "is first a temper, and then a place." To be good, then, a man must share in this temper; it is not enough that he does his duty, that he is strict in his obedience to the moral law; he must not be sour about it. A good man must not merely strike us with awe and reverence; he must attract our love and admiration.[8] This is excellent admonition, but it can be treacherous. When Whichcote remarks in a sermon that "a good man is an instrument in tune,"[9] he is very near to explaining virtue as a natural and spontaneous activity. When attacking Hobbism and Calvinism it was easy to go to the opposite extreme.

For many reasons the spirit of the age was moving in this direction. From the Anglican pulpits there be-

gan to come sermons in a new style, with no mention
of the vessel of dung or the sink of iniquity. Gregory
Hascard said in a sermon in 1685:

> When our tempers are soft and sensible, and easily receive
> impressions from the sufferings of others, we are pained
> within, and to ease our selves, we are ready to succour them,
> and then Nature discharging her Burthen and Oppression,
> creates both her own pleasure and satisfaction, and performs
> her Duty.

In 1697 a higher authority, the eminent William Sher-
lock, dean of St. Paul's, preached the same doctrine:

> A soft and tender mind, which feels the sufferings of
> others, and suffers with them, is the true temper and spirit
> of charity; and Nature prompts us to ease those sufferings
> which we feel. . . . An inward Principle is more powerful
> than all external arguments; and Sense and Feeling is this
> Principle, and Charity is this Sense.

We may observe more than one new element in these
two passages. First, we find Nature, with a capital letter, prompting us, and Nature creating her pleasure
and performing her duty. If we will allow her, Nature
will come to our assistance in a situation in which we
have to make a moral choice. Nature will ease the
choice. But Nature can do her beneficent work best if
our tempers are soft and sensible, if our minds are
tender. And the virtue these preachers are most interested in is charity, unselfishness, help to the distressed.
These three new elements point forward directly to
some of the main characteristics of European thought

in the next hundred years. The good preachers could
of course never have suspected that; but we can see it
in retrospect.

If one presses a little too much the idea that virtue is
accompanied by pleasure, one lapses into hedonism.
There were moments when the divines of the seventeenth century seemed bent on presenting the tempta-
tion to virtue as even more seductive than the tempta-
tion to vice. Isaac Barrow, professor of Greek at Cambridge and a distinguished divine, wrote in 1671 that
an unselfish act is accompanied by what he calls a
"very delicious relish," and he goes on to say that "a
man may be virtuously voluptuous, and a laudable epi-
cure by doing much good." Even Archbishop Tillotson
thought that "there is no sensual pleasure in the world
comparable to the delight and satisfaction that a good
man takes in doing good." Richard Kidder said that
"there is a delight and joy that accompanies doing
good, there is a kind of sensuality in it." [10] We may
agree that these worthy divines were getting close to a
certain truth; there is a pleasure—if one wants to call
it that, though happiness might be a better term—in a
moral life; there is a joy in it. But to speak of sensuality and sensual pleasure and epicurism is to confuse
two levels of our consciousness and to reduce the moral
impulse to do good with such impulses as are properly
called appetites. It is obvious what such language leads
to in the moral analysis of human nature. After 1700,
when benevolence or unselfishness came to be spoken
of more and more as the chief virtue, and even as the

source of all the other virtues, it was referred to as the "social passions" or the "social affections," and that man was thought to come nearest to moral perfection whose goodness was grounded in his passionate nature.

The portrait of the virtuous man according to this pattern has been drawn for us by a multitude of writers of the eighteenth century. They first called him a man of sensibility. About 1740 a new word was coined to describe him, *sentimental,* and modern scholars, whose occupation is the study of *isms,* call the whole movement, which swept all Europe as well as England, the age of sentimentalism. The tone of literature and society had changed profoundly in the first half of the eighteenth century. In 1749 a lady of quality wrote a letter to the great novelist Richardson, from which we learn that the word *sentimental* was then in constant use among her friends; everything good and pleasant was sentimental; they took sentimental walks, they had sentimental conversations; she begged him to explain the meaning of the word which seemed to embrace everything that is good. Richardson's reply, if he sent one, has not come down to us; but his three lengthy novels are among the greatest as well as most characteristic products of the whole sentimental movement. To use the language of eulogy of that time, the magic skill of Richardson now melts us with pity, now thrills us with anguish, with a sort of pleasing anguish that sweetly melts the mind. A disposition to tears was not only a proof of a genuine moral sensibility; it was itself an exercise in virtue, a moral conditioning of the

heart. James Thomson thought that Nature had be-
stowed upon man this prerogative above all other animals that he alone could weep.[11] When even a general
wept over a tender scene in Sir Richard Steele's comedy, *The Conscious Lovers* (1722), Steele came to his
defense in his preface to the play. "I must contend,"
he observed, "that men ought not to be laughed at for
weeping till we are come to a more clear notion of what
is to be imputed to the hardness of the head and the
softness of the heart. . . . To be apt to give way to the
impressions of humanity is the excellence of a right
disposition and the natural working of a well-turned
spirit." In France they were also beginning to soften
the heart with the new-style weeping comedy, which
they termed *la comédie larmoyante*. The novel, of
course, became tearful at the same time as the drama,
and with few exceptions the European novelists of the
eighteenth century aimed at exciting this sweet and
virtuous sensibility. The flood of Richardsonian imita-
tions was especially welcomed by the young ladies,
and they were rapturously described in the prologue
to George Colman's *Honeycombe* (1760):

> And then so sentimental is the style,
> So chaste yet so bewitching all the while!
> Plot and elopement, passion, rape, and rapture,
> The total sum of ev'ry dear—dear—chapter.

The new circulating libraries made this profusion of
sentimental fiction available to every young devotee
such as Miss Lydia Languish in Sheridan's play.

The poets were equally diligent in exploring the possibilities of the sentimental life. As the prosaic happenings of daily existence are likely to grate on truly delicate sensibilities, the poets began to seek solitude. A lonely evening walk away from the busy hum of men could offer the poet the opportunity to converse with Nature, there to harmonize his heart, to "solitary court the inspiring breeze, and meditate the book of Nature, ever open, aiming thence warm from the heart to learn the moral song." [12] The sweetest of moods was Melancholy, Queen of Thought, associated most often, naturally, with night. Her the poetic votary might woo at twilight hour beneath the moss-grown piles of a ruined abbey, with the pale moon pouring her long-leveled streaming light, while all around a sacred sullen silence reigns save the lone screech-owl's note, who builds her bower in the moldering caverns dark and deep. Toward midnight the poet might wander about in the gloomy void and feel religious horror wrap his soul in dread repose. After midnight he could visit the hollow charnel with its stacks of old bones, and with a dim and flickering taper watch the ghostly shapes of the shadows as they seemed to invite with beckoning hand his lonesome steps through the far-winding vaults. The poet would, however, not use this occasion for a Hamlet-like realization of the transitoriness of life and the inevitability of death. Such gross and severe reflections would have been out of tune with sweet sensibility enjoying the pleasures of melancholy.[13]

But we must not linger over these literary aspects of the sentimental movement. In themselves they were pleasant enough and we may share a taste for some of them, for moments of solitude, for communing with Nature, or even for a midnight visit to the graveyard with the moon setting and the owl hooting from the ivy-covered tower. As a matter of fact, from this poetry of thrilling horror came the Gothic novel of the eighteenth century, and from the Gothic novel came the stories of Edgar Allan Poe, and from them in turn came the modern detective story, so that we should all be grateful to the melancholy sentimentalists of the eighteenth century for their exploitation of these thrills. But in our present investigation we are concerned with a more serious matter. For at the core of the whole sentimental movement, in England, in France, in all Europe, we find a set of doctrines; we find a psychological theory, an ethical theory, a theory regarding the nature of man. All these theories are so closely interdependent that the acceptance of any one must imply the acceptance of the others.

The most influential exponent, but not, as has sometimes been contended, the originator, of these theories was undoubtedly Anthony Ashley Cooper, the third Earl of Shaftesbury, whose *Characteristics* were published in three stately volumes in 1711, beautiful books that would adorn any gentleman's library. The Earl had enjoyed a most remarkable education. He was not sent to public school or to a university, but was educated at home under a tutor who taught him in his ten-

der years to speak as well as read Greek and Latin; as
a result he was even as an adolescent living in easy
familiarity with the great ancient classics. From childhood he seems to have been a discriminating rather
than an omnivorous reader. It was his observation
later in life that they who read many books must of
necessity read more bad books than good—a proposition that would be difficult to controvert. He early discovered his favorites, such as Plato, Cicero, Marcus
Aurelius, and among the moderns the Cambridge Platonists. As his constitution was sickly, he spent many
years in Italy, where he profited by his opportunity to
cultivate a discerning taste in painting, sculpture, and
architecture. Altogether he appears to have been a very
attractive person, with the noble and generous sentiments, and also the prejudices, of a very finely educated gentleman. Not that he was snobbish in the vulgar
sense; we may be sure that he would have cordially
appreciated nobility of character in any man, with or
without an escutcheon. But there were classes of people
whom he despised—among them the pedants of the
universities. Most of all he had a contempt for those
hard and thick-skinned people who are incapable, and
are content to remain incapable, of generous responses
to the good and the beautiful. All such people lack good
breeding.

There has been some dispute in the past as to the
exact nature of Shaftesbury's philosophical drift. He
did not write a systematic treatise, such as would be
required from a professor or a pedant, but easy and

informal gentlemanly essays, in which he made statements of various and even contradictory tendencies. It
is possible to extract from his volumes passages to
show that he was a Stoic like Marcus Aurelius, or that
he was a Platonist or a Ciceronian. It is even possible
to find in various places the main ideas of the doctrine
of the Law of Nature. But it was not what Shaftesbury
had in common with Marcus Aurelius or Cicero that
made readers of the eighteenth century buy edition
after edition of his work, or that brought him so many
notable philosophical disciples in and out of the universities. What captured the eighteenth century was
his view of the natural goodness of human nature, an
innate disposition to virtue such as could be corrupted
only by evil custom or education. Man has in his nature, Shaftesbury said, a "moral sense," a sort of
sixth sense comparable to the other senses, by which
he may perceive spontaneously and surely the difference between right and wrong. This moral sense was
not the same as the familiar old concept of the conscience or the Ciceronian idea of right reason; it became the substitute for them. The moral sense operates
like the other senses, and Shaftesbury liked to speak
of it as an inner taste—a taste for the good, the true,
and the beautiful. Psychologically, it is the true inward
source of good conduct. " 'Tis not merely what we call
principle," he says, "but a taste which governs men."
We may think for certain that one thing is right and
another wrong, yet, as he says, "if the savor of things
lies cross to honesty," conduct will inevitably go the

wrong way. "Even conscience, I fear, such as is owing to religious discipline, will make but a slight figure where this taste is amiss." What then is a good man? A good man is a man of finely cultivated tastes, in morals as well as in art, whose personality is so harmoniously developed that the unfolding of it reveals the good that is naturally in his nature. This is the way of true philosophy. For to philosophize, he explains, "in a just signification, is but to carry good-breeding a step higher. For the accomplishment of breeding is to learn whatever is decent in company or beautiful in arts; and the sum of philosophy is to learn what is just in society and beautiful in Nature and the order of the world." [14]

The best we can say about this as a philosophy of morals is that it attempts to lay the foundations of morality in the depths of the nature of the individual, as also did Cicero, the Law of Nature, and the Cambridge Platonists; the worst is that, in so doing, it eliminates the conscience with its authority, and the right reason with its universality. It relies on the impulses and instincts, on what the poets called "the social passions" and the "social affections," or on what Adam Smith, professor of moral philosophy at Glasgow, called "the moral sentiments," to guide human nature in all the problems of moral conduct. Shaftesbury himself sometimes anticipated the very turns of expression of the later sentimentalists, as when he wrote to a young Oxford student :"Be persuaded, that wisdom is more from the heart than from the head. Feel goodness, and you will see all things fair and good."

Thus the authority of the conscience, the imperative
of the moral judgment, is left out of the conception of
human nature. Rousseau, always responsive to the
sentimental developments of his time and a supreme
exponent of them, is explicit and firm on this point; he
wrote fine declamations in praise of the conscience, the
divine gift in the heart of man, but he repeatedly denied that conscience is anything but an emotion or feeling. Man is by nature good; he is corrupted only by
external influences. His salvation is in following nature, that is, his own nature, his own organic impulses
and appetites, in developing to fruition and complete-
ness his natural humanity. This is nature's simple plan.
Already in 1723 Mandeville had observed that Shaftesbury "imagines that men without any trouble or violence upon themselves may be naturally virtuous. He
seems to require and expect goodness in his species, as
we do a sweet taste in grapes and China oranges, of
which, if any of them are sour, we boldly pronounce
that they are not come to that perfection their nature
is capable of." [15] Mandeville's sarcasm happens to
underscore the psychology and ethics of the forward-
looking movement in Europe for the next seventy-five
years.

It was with this dominant movement that Helvetius
collided when he published his *De l'esprit* in 1758. His
description of man as absolutely and inescapably selfish was a throwback to Hobbes, whose ideas on this
matter had by this time been universally rejected even
by the *philosophes*. Helvetius was probably unable con-

stitutionally to appreciate the generosity of sentiment
in the new movement around him. He was not a typical
man of sensibility. When he died in 1771 the imagination of Europe had already been captured by such en-
thusiasts as Diderot and Rousseau, and German Ro-
manticism was entranced by the idea of the beautiful
soul, *die schöne Seele*. But not all of the ideas of
Helvetius suffered such eclipse. His critics agreed with
him about the materialistic universe presented by the
science of Newton, and they accepted as basic truth
the psychology of Locke. And somehow they had to
manage to reconcile this science with their enthusiasm
over the natural goodness of man. The solution to this
problem they believed they had found in the distinction
between Nature and art, between Nature and civilization. The salvation of man lay in following Nature.

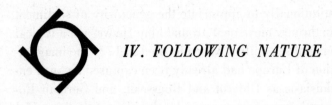 *IV. FOLLOWING NATURE*

The adage that we should follow Nature is so ancient and so widely popular that it seems like a bit of folklore. As a matter of fact it is a rather specific philosophical dogma which we have inherited from Graeco-Roman civilization. It still seems to preserve for the most part the character of moral exhortation, applicable when we are faced with a choice of conduct. In our daily speech we do not usually turn to it as a scientific formula, as a caution, for instance, to a man who tries to make water run uphill. Following Nature has with the centuries become a precept, not of science, but of wisdom, especially of moral wisdom. It has become a part of the vernacular moral vocabulary of Europe.

The origin of this idea is a difficult study requiring special erudition. We cannot pause over the early philosophical gropings which first called the cosmic process Nature and then hypostatized a Nature of meaning and spirit and values which could be at the same time within the cosmic process and distinct from it. We have seen how Heraclitus concluded that there must be some divine Logos which is the original of Justice. Since this aspiration, this need for a life of right reason, is a part of our human nature, there must be something correspondent to it in the universe. It therefore seemed to some ancient thinkers that there must be a rationality in the cosmic process, a principle that could hold the universe together in a sense beyond the mere materialistic. This principle the Stoics called Nature. The soul must rise to lofty heights to understand and realize such a conception. "I am in harmony with all that is a part of thy harmony, great Universe," said Marcus Aurelius. "He who knows not the world-order, knows not his own place therein. And he who knows not for what he exists, knows not himself nor the world." The health of the soul and by consequence the happiness of man lies in conformity to this ideal world. "For every living thing," said Epictetus, "was so framed by Nature as to flee and turn from things, and the causes of things, that appear hurtful, and admire things, and the causes of things, that appear serviceable." These ideas about Nature are familiar to readers of the later Stoics, Marcus Aurelius, Epictetus, and Seneca. But they were developed by Roman Stoicism even before Cicero, and his formulation of them incorporated them into the body of later European ethical and legal theory, as we have already seen in connection with the history of the Law of Nature. The Law of Nature could have no philosophical meaning except in the context of such an ideal Nature. In order to affirm that virtue is an ultimate and self-authenticating value, Cicero says that it is good, even if it were commended by no one, because it is good by Nature (*honestum . . . etiamsi a nullo laudetur, natura esse laudabile*).[1] Nature is thus conceivable as a source of both morality and law.

"Law is the distinction between the just and the unjust as expressed in conformity with that first and most ancient of all things, Nature." [2] Such was the moral tone, such the *dogmata*, from which emerged the ancient precept that we should Follow Nature.

But *Nature*, as we have already observed in our discussion of the Law of Nature, is a difficult term to control. Speculation can move out from it in several directions. As used in our moral precept it designates a norm or standard for the moral judgment; it expresses an *ought* which may be, and usually is, quite distinct and even alien from what *is*. But it seems reasonable to assume that this normative meaning could have occurred to the human mind only after the word *Nature* had become familiar in its purely descriptive meaning, referring to nothing beyond factual phenomena. This is the meaning of Nature lodged in the popular mind of modern times, and many people consequently have great difficulty in apprehending that the laws of nature as exemplified in chemistry and physics refer to one kind of reality, but that the Law of Nature as a principle of justice and right refers to any reality at all. It seems so much more intelligible to say, for instance, that when we take advantage of our knowledge of physiology and pathology to improve our health, we are in this manner really Following Nature. There is even the possibility of setting up this descriptive concept as itself a norm in opposition to a normative Nature, as when satirists down through the ages and sociologists in more recent times testify that monogamy is an un-

successful institution and should therefore be abandoned as unnatural. Or the inference may be made that
the *homme moyen sensuel* is the natural man, whose
proclivities should not only be accepted and tolerated,
but even set up as a more natural standard or norm.
All the danger and uneasiness of moral overstrain
could thus be eliminated, and one would still be Following Nature. Finally, this descriptive notion of natural man can be opposed to custom and "artificial" society, and thus, again raised to a norm, become the
central doctrine of an attack on civilization or even a
program for revolution. That, also, may be called Following Nature.

All these varieties of opposition to the normative
conception of Nature were put forward already in ancient times and are not unfamiliar to readers of Plato
and Cicero. But in modern times, since the Renaissance, and especially in the Enlightenment, they have
advanced in popularity and prestige from the status
of notorious heresies to become the orthodox tenets of
advanced thinkers. They acquired a new vitality from
the two developments we have discussed, the scientific
study of man and the sentimental belief in the natural
goodness of man. Each of these attempted to interpret
from its own assumptions the principle that we should
Follow Nature. Curiously enough, they converged and
reinforced one another.

As we have already seen, the scientific students of
human nature, following Hobbes, generally committed
themselves to reducing man to a machine, and the prob-

lem of ethics and social science would therefore be to
learn how to manage such a machine. On this basis the
management of education, society, and government
should, in theory at least, not be difficult, providing we
overlook the initial difficulty of the theory that the
moralists, the philosophers, and the legislators, who
are to do the managing, must also be machines. Those
who have had experience in such matters will assure
us that machines cannot be repaired by machines, but
only by the intervention of human ingenuity. The mar-
velous mechanical brains of our day have to be operated by human intelligence; as an expert on them has
warned us, they are not brains at all, but only mechanical memories. But let us pass over this difficulty. Let
us assume that our study of man is to be strictly scientific. We can, in the twentieth century, refine immensely
on the crude psychology of Hobbes. Even the philosophers of the eighteenth century knew more than he
about physiology and anatomy. They based their psychology on Locke, who had certainly improved greatly
on that of Hobbes. But whatever progress they made in
observation and experiment, their science remained
science, that is, a description of facts or supposed facts.
Such a scientific study of human nature presumably
discovers the laws by which human nature operates, as
a scientific study of a gasoline engine discovers its
peculiar laws of operation. Are these the laws that are
to supersede the old-fashioned moral laws? Are these
laws of nature to be the guides in human conduct in
the new age? The *philosophes* liked to think so. They

liked to consider man as part of physical nature, as operating under the same kind of law. They would have been reluctant to agree with Emerson's dictum that there is one law for man and one for thing. Diderot was thinking of moral commands when he observed that "you may command what is contrary to nature, but you will never be obeyed." The conclusion must be that moral science should follow nature in this special sense that it will not issue commands which will not be obeyed. Obviously, when moral science in this way loses its normative character, it ceases to be moral. Bishop Butler protested against this absurdity already in a sermon in 1726, when he said that if by following Nature we merely mean that we shall behave as we necessarily must, there is no meaning in saying that we *must* or *should* follow Nature, as moralists have been saying ever since Aristotle.

But this idea of Nature as referring to obstinate facts and actualities could be put to a variety of uses. The philosophers of the eighteenth century were dedicated to a renovation of the world and to giving humanity a fresh start. They engaged in a great critical examination of the traditions and institutions and practices of civilization, to test their soundness and validity, to determine which should be abandoned and what new institutions and practices should take their place. They found, alas, a whole mass of restrictive regulations, oppressive institutions, irritating and tormenting duties and obligations, which, to borrow the phrase of Shaftesbury, had a savor cross to the inclinations of man. All of these could be declared evil because they did not follow Nature, because they violated the first principle that you must not command what is contrary to Nature or you will not be obeyed. You will only multiply evildoers, said Diderot. All this rubbish must be cleared away and a society established on new principles soundly based on a knowledge of man as he is by nature.

What kind of creature is this natural man? Is he good or bad or a mixture of both qualities? If the answer is that he is not virtuous by nature but completely selfish, one is propelled in the direction of the abhorrent political absolutism of Hobbes or the absolute bureaucracy of Helvetius. But the development of sentimentalism had taught the philosophers that man is naturally good and that what we find evil in him must be due to external influences, specifically the evil institutions, practices, and traditions that people called civilization. Everything was good as it came from the hand of God and Nature, said Rousseau, everything deteriorates in the hands of man. The question naturally presents itself how man, if he is naturally good, managed to overwhelm himself with all these wicked institutions? A philosopher would blame the priests, or the politicians, or whoever happened to be the object of his special animus. Looking further into this problem would seem to him unprofitable. Let us therefore pass this over also for the moment. But it is important for us to observe that the sentimental view of human nature as naturally good became the indispensable assumption in the schemes of the scientific social engineers of the period. That is what we find in Diderot in France and Godwin in England. There were some exceptions; there were scientists like Helvetius who were not men of much sentiment; there were men of sensibility like Rousseau who were indifferent about the scientific method. But the great revolutionary movement of the century was sustained and invigorated by these two modes of thought and feeling. They reinforced each other. They led to the same conclusion regarding the meaning of the expression, "Let us follow Nature."

In general the effect of this development was to release the human organism from the control of any social inheritance, and internally to release the instinctive and emotional propensities from control by reflective principle. Cicero presented the idea of Nature as a norm or standard, as a system of values apprehended by Right Reason; the positivists reduced Nature to a descriptive term referring to what is or must be, not to what ought to be. Following Nature in that sense obviously involves no inner struggle, no inner compulsion. Wherever a conflict appears between natural man and the customs, morals, or institutions, all of these must be abandoned as not following Nature. Sentimentalism led to the same conclusion by appealing to the natural goodness of our inner feelings, instincts, and organic needs. When Antigone in the play by Sophocles had violated the king's decree she appealed to a law higher and more sacred than any decree by man:

> Not of to-day or yesterday
> Is this a law, but ever hath it life,
> And no man knoweth whence it came or how.

As has been understood from Aristotle down to modern times, Antigone is here appealing to a universal and over-individual Law of Nature, to eternal laws of justice. But Kotzebue, a German dramatist whose plays were popular all over Europe toward the end of the eighteenth century, happened to provide an instructive modern contrast to Antigone. The infraction of his heroine is defended by the current doctrine that the time for compulsive laws and institutions is over; with the passage of centuries of time the *laws* of propriety have now been transformed into a *feeling* for propriety. "Eine lange Reihe von Jahren hat das Gesetz des Schicklichen in das Gefühl des Schicklichen verwandelt." [3] History and experience, as well as rational inference, indicate that such theory leads to extreme individualism, to perpetual protest against all tradition, to the rejection of anything that is inhibiting or contrary to our natural impulses. It sets up a profound opposition between Nature and civilization.

But history and experience seemed to the *philosophes* to teach that this opposition must be overcome by the complete triumph of Nature:

Shall I outline for you the historical origin of nearly all of our unhappiness? [Diderot asked.] It is simply this: Once upon a time there was a natural man; then an artificial man was built up inside him. Since then a civil war has been raging continuously within his breast. Sometimes the natural man proves stronger; at other times he is laid low by the artificial, moral man [*l'homme moral et artificiel*]. But whichever gains the upper hand, the poor freak is racked and torn, tortured, stretched on the wheel, continually suffering, continually wretched, whether because he is out of his senses with some misplaced passion for glory or because imaginary shame curbs him and bows him down. But in spite of all this, there are occasions when man recovers his original simplicity under the pressure of extreme necessity.[4]

Such convulsions within the heart of man were quite unnecessary. They could be eliminated by an enlightened social science. Abolish the artificial man who is formed by customs, institutions, and prejudices, re-educate a generation or two, and the human race will enjoy the universal happiness for which it was intended by Nature. What causes the unfaithfulness of husband and wife? The institution of marriage; abolish marriage and there will be no unfaithfulness. Who wages wars? Kings do; let us abolish monarchy and wars will cease. The evil that humanity suffers from is somehow between men, not within them. It can be traced to the church, or to government, or to aristocracy, or to monogamy, or to the schools, or to eating meat, and so forth.

The eighteenth century consequently looked with expectant eagerness for examples of man living in the state of nature, or nearly so. Their search was rewarded with many discoveries, only a few of which we have time to examine.

One of the persistent preoccupations of the period was the search for the spontaneous and preferably uneducated poetic genius. By 1750 there had developed in England a reaction against the Classical poetry of Dryden, Pope, and the other writers of the heroic couplet. Pope had expressed the creed of the Classical school in terms of following an ideal Nature, what the French called *la belle Nature:*

> First follow Nature, and your judgment frame
> By her just standard, which is still [ever] the same:
> Unerring Nature, still divinely bright,
> One clear, unchanged, and universal light,
> Life, force, and beauty, must to all impart.

But the young men of the century considered such a precept conducive to nothing but artificiality. In a poem called *The Enthusiast,* written in 1744, Joseph Warton asked:

> What are the lays of artful Addison,
> Coldly correct, to Shakespeare's warblings wild?

Warton and others began to range Dryden and Pope in the second order of poetry, and chose Shakespeare, Spenser, and Milton to represent poetry of the highest order. In this ranking they were certainly correct. But they insisted also on a theory that opposed the poetry of nature to the poetry of art. The poets of art, skilled craftsmen like Virgil and Ben Jonson, labored over

their verses until they were coldly correct. But the
poets of nature, like Homer in the morning of the
world or gentle Shakespeare, "nature's child," war-
bled their songs as wildly and spontaneously as birds.
In Germany Herder developed this opposition into a
formula for *Kulturgeschichte;* he contrasted two kinds
of poetry, *Kunstpoesie* and *Volkspoesie. Volkspoesie,*
spontaneous poetry springing from the breasts of the
people themselves, was thought to be such poetry as the
medieval ballads of England, or the medieval German
poetry dealing with the legends of the German gods,
or the Old Norse poetry composed by Skalds, who
seemed to the eighteenth century to have been primitive men, bards by Nature's gift and uncontaminated
by art. The ancient bard, as described even by Thomas
Gray, who was himself a cultivated and fastidious
classicist, illustrates, he says, the "extensive influence
of poetic genius over the remotest and most uncivilized
nations." In Lapland, he says in his poem, the Muse
has broke the twilight gloom, and among the Indians
of Chili's boundless forests She also

> deigns to hear the savage youth repeat
> In loose numbers wildly sweet
> Their feather-cinctured chiefs and dusky loves.

But if there were poets by nature among the Lap-
landers and the Indians of Chile, should there not be
natural geniuses also right at home among the uneducated people of England? In their state of eagerness
and expectancy, the educated readers and patrons of

poetry discovered a whole series of them. There was, first, Stephen Duck, the poetical thresherman, whose story is told on the title page which he himself wrote for the 1753 edition of his poems. He was for many years "a poor thresher in a barn at Charleton in the county of Wilts, at the wages of four shillings and sixpence per week, till taken notice of by her late Majesty, Queen Caroline; who, on account of his great genius, gave him an apartment at Kew and a salary of thirty pounds per annum; after which he studied the learned languages, took orders, and is now a dignified clergyman." The effort to live up to his exalted status and his great reputation proved to be too much for him, his mind gave way, and he drowned himself in the Thames. Mary Collier, the poetical washerwoman of Peterfield, published a poem in 1739, reprinted in 1762. But she failed to get distinguished patronage. More fortunate was Henry Jones, the poetical bricklayer of Dublin, who was discovered by no less a person than the elegant Earl of Chesterfield, who brought Jones to England and made him a member of his household. But Jones took to drink, got involved financially with other servants, was dismissed by the Earl, was run over in Saint Martin's Lane while drunk, and died a few days later in the parish workhouse. Then there was James Woodhouse, the poetical shoemaker, to whom Dr. Johnson gave the advice that he should stick to his last. Finally, there was Ann Yearsley, the poetical milk or pig woman of Bristol who in 1783 was taken under the patronage of the learned ladies who were called the

Blue Stockings. The list of subscribers to the printing of her poems included such names as Mrs. Montagu, Mrs. Delany, Mrs. Boscawen, the Duchess of Devonshire, the Duchess of Beaufort, and the Duchess of Portland. "Indeed, she is one of Nature's miracles," exclaimed Mrs. Montagu. "What harmony of numbers! What force of imagination! Wonder not, if our humble dame rises above Pindar or steps beyond Aeschylus." But Ann Yearsley soon quarreled with her benefactors over the money they raised for her, the bubble reputation burst, and the pig woman returned to her pig and obscurity. Three years later, in 1786, when Robert Burns published his first volume of poetry, the reviewers of London and Edinburgh hailed him as another child of nature, a poet without art or education, although, as we now know, he was highly educated in his calling, and the inheritor of centuries of Scottish poetical tradition.[5]

Joseph Warton indulged in a little myth to explain the genius of Shakespeare: Fair Fancy found him as a smiling babe on winding Avon's willowed banks and carried him off to a close cavern where he listened with deep delight to her songs. And before Warton the pride of England was hailed by James Thomson in these terms:

Is not wild Shakespeare thine and nature's boast? [6]

These were the commonplaces of English thought many years before Rousseau in 1762 published his *Emile*, which was to become the classic on education

according to Nature. Rousseau explains that in this
fictional biography of an orphan boy he wants to *form*
the man of nature, a paradox which disappears when
he further states that this forming means the elimina-
tion from the experience of the child of all influence by
civil society. In his novel he provides a tutor for Emile,
but the effort of the tutor is to be purely negative. He is
to see to it that nothing interferes with the spontaneous
development of the senses and faculties of the pupil.
Let the boy form his own course; let him see with his
own eyes, feel according to his own heart, let him be
governed by no authority except that of his own intelligence. There must be no instruction; Emile must learn
everything by observation and experience. He must
not see a book until after the age of twelve, and his first
reading is to be *Robinson Crusoe*. He must learn astronomy by getting lost in the woods and finding the polar
star; he must learn geometry without book, that is, he
must be an adolescent Euclid. If he breaks the window
of his room, let him learn from experience what it is
like to live with bad weather beating in. The reader of
*Emile* may be excused for pitying this poor unloved
boy who so desperately needed a mother's care. All
through his childhood and youth he has no companion-
ship except with this uncommunicative tutor who offers
no help other than secretly arranging situations by
which the boy may learn from experience, but who
will otherwise instruct him in nothing.

Emile, however, had at least a tutor; as he grew up
he saw one human being other than himself. But in

1763, only the next year after the appearance of Rousseau's book, another philosopher of the Parisian group, Beaurieu, gave the world an improvement even on *Emile*. He called his story *The Pupil of Nature*. To preserve his hero in a state of absolutely uncontaminated Nature Beaurieu had him confined for the first fifteen years of his life in a wooden cage, in which he was fed by persons he never saw and in which he never heard the sound of human voice. He could therefore be guaranteed free from corruption by human society. As an adolescent he was transported in some way to an uninhabited island, again without seeing or hearing the human beings who transported him. He was then ready to begin his life as a true child of Nature. In this pure and pristine condition he proceeded to learn everything he needed to know, including geometry and botany and the existence and nature of God. This was education according to Nature.

These absurdities were of course intended to emphasize the important underlying principle that all education is in a sense self-education. This is no doubt an acceptable principle, provided it is properly qualified. But if it is joined with a sublime confidence in the native intellectual capacity and innate goodness of human nature, if it is to deprive the child of his rightful inheritance from the society into which he is born, if he is not to be fed intellectually or given any bringing-up in conduct, then, it would seem, the theory can become very dangerous indeed. When Aristotle lectured on ethics to the young men of Athens he told

them that it is useless to lecture on ethics to young men
unless they have been properly brought up. To the uncontaminated child of Nature Aristotle on ethics would
ever remain a sealed book.

As we have seen, the uneducated poets of the century
were disappointments. The children in the educational
novels were fictitious and unreal. But since the sixteenth century Europe had been finding actual noble
savages in various parts of the world. And the eighteenth century was thrilled to discover the finest speci-
mens of them all in the islands of the South Pacific,
genuine children of Nature, whose life was so primitive
and so idyllic as to match the fabled Golden Age and to
suggest the way to a new Golden Age in the future.
About 1769 the French Admiral Bougainville, in a
voyage around the world, discovered Tahiti. In 1771
he published his narrative of the voyage, a factual account such as one would expect from a naval officer
making a report. Denis Diderot, the central figure
among the Parisian philosophers, felt that the Admiral
had missed a great philosophical opportunity, and he
immediately wrote what he called a *Supplement to the
Voyages of Bougainville*. Briefly described, it is another one of those dialogues, not uncommon in the
eighteenth century, between a European and a savage,
each defending his own morals and way of life, with
the savage always winning the victory. Diderot under-
takes to give a full narrative of incidents which the
Admiral had naturally suppressed in his own account
of his visits and conversations with the natives. Dide-

rot has the native Chief Orou explain the complete and
ideal freedom of the sexes in this isle of Cytherea. This
is too much for the chaplain, who is of course a Catholic priest and whose sense of duty impels him to en-
lighten the chief regarding the ordinances of the holy
institution of matrimony. Diderot, hating all Catholic
priests, adds some farce to the situation which makes
the holy man quite ridiculous. But the issues are too
serious for mere farce. The noble figure of Chief Orou
raises the tone to an appropriate and edifying level.
He asks some searching questions about conditions in
France, especially about how monogamy works out, to
which the embarrassed priest could make only falter-
ing answers. The keen savage soon sees through it all:

What a monstrous tissue is this that thou are unfolding
to me! And even now thou dost not tell me all; for as soon
as men allow themselves to dispose at their own will of the
ideas of what is just and unjust, to take away, or to impose
an arbitrary character on things; to unite to actions or to
separate from them the good, and the evil, with no coun-
sellor save caprice—then come blame, accusation, suspicion,
tyranny, envy, jealousy, deception, chagrin, concealment,
dissimulation, espionage, surprise, lies; daughters deceive
their parents, wives their husbands, husbands their wives;
young women, I don't doubt, will smother their children;
suspicious fathers will despise and neglect their children;
mothers will leave them to the mercy of accident; and crime
and debauchery will show themselves in every guise. I know
all that, as if I had lived among you. It is so, because it must
be so; and that society of thine, in spite of thy chief who
vaunts its fine order, is nothing but a collection of hypocrites
who secretly trample the laws under foot; or of unfortunate

wretches who make themselves the instrument of their own punishment; or of imbeciles, in whom prejudice has absolutely stifled the voice of nature.[7]

One observes first with some surprise how adequate the vocabulary of the happy isle is to describe the horrors of depraved civilization. But the savage chief was not limited to denunciation; in his primal innocence he could also grasp and express philosophical principles and argue from them, principles which, by a happy coincidence, were precisely those held by Diderot. He pronounces them eloquently:

These singular precepts I find opposed to nature and contrary to reason. They are contrary to nature because they suppose that a being who thinks, feels, and is free, can be the property of a creature like itself. . . . And they are contrary to the general law of things. Can anything seem more senseless to thee than a precept which proscribes the law of change that is within us, and which commands a constancy that is impossible, and that violates the liberty of the male and the female, by chaining them together in perpetuity;—anything more senseless than are oaths of immutability, taken by two creatures of flesh, in the face of a sky that is not an instant the same, under vaults that threaten ruin, at the base of a rock crumbling to dust, at the foot of a tree that is splitting asunder? . . . You may command what is opposed to nature, but you will not be obeyed. You will multiply evil-doers and the unhappy by fear, by punishment, by remorse; you will deprave men's consciences; you will corrupt their minds; they will have lost the polar star of their pathway.[8]

This is of course Diderot himself speaking. He was an enthusiast and given to such outbursts of *Schwärmerei*.

In his excitement he borrows the conscience and the polar star from the language of those moralists who were following a different Nature from his. It must be granted that Diderot was not entirely insincere about that; ethics was also one of his life-long enthusiasms, and he always hoped that he could write a treatise demonstrating that virtue is preferable to vice. But he explained himself that he was always perplexed by a demon of philosophy which convinced him that the only sound basis for morals was science, especially physiology and medicine. Over this contradiction he agonized. He was profoundly moved by the fate of Seneca, who suffered martyrdom at the orders of Nero; he shed tears over Seneca, as he did over many another character in history, fiction, and real life. Is it not possible, he wrote in his commentary on Seneca, that it would be better to suffer martyrdom with Seneca than to be the cruel tyrant who inflicted it? Oh, I believe it, I believe it: *Je le crois, je le crois.* He felt with his whole nature the greatness of a good deed or a good sentiment. But he could not escape consulting science also. And search as one might in the books on physiology or medicine, nothing appeared there to justify martyrdom.

This difficulty Diderot was never able to overcome. He could never reach a philosophy of human nature which distinguished between moral force and material force, between the imperative of a moral judgment and the physical necessity of a scientific physiology and neurology.[9] He was therefore unable to hold fast to any

meaningful concept of the conscience which should not
be depraved. When Diderot was still a youth Bishop
Butler had said in the second of his *Sermons upon
Human Nature* (1726) that conscience means direction
and superintendency; "to preside and govern, from the
very economy and constitution of man, belongs to it.
Had it strength, as it has right; had it power, as it has
manifest authority, it would absolutely govern the
world." Butler expressed the paradox and mystery of
our moral freedom and moral responsibility, factors
of our common experience which are not reducible to
scientific statement. Diderot's eloquent apostrophe to
the polar star and the conscience therefore comes down
at last only to this maxim, that commands should not
be issued if they are going to be disobeyed; let man
follow the impulses of his nature, as the rivulet finds
its course around obstructions down to the sea.

One more precept of the noble chief of Tahiti must
be examined: that we must not violate the law of change
which is within us as well as everywhere observable in
the cosmos about us. This idea has been dear to the
modern world since the seventeenth century. It was an
important part of the great ground swell which has
shifted European thought. It provided a sort of scientific sanction to the religion of the complete man, the
free and complete expansion of *die Menschlichkeit*.
John Dewey, a modern of the moderns, has somewhere
remarked that perhaps the single moral end, if there
is one, is "growth." Whether the growth is beneficent
or malign would therefore be impossible to decide on

ethical grounds, for if growth is itself the ultimate value, all growth must be assumed to be good. How distinctively modern such thinking is we begin to realize when we search for anything like it in the great writers of the sixteenth century. Spenser, for instance, began his poetical career writing about the Ruins of Rome and the Ruins of Time, borrowing these themes from the French poets before him. Behold Rome, he wrote,

> what wrack, what ruin, and what waste,
> And how that she, which with her mighty power
> Tamed all the world, hath tamed herself at last,
> The prey of Time, which all things doth devour.

The poetry of Spenser is the expression of the longing of man—immersed as he is in a world of perpetual change and subject himself in large degree to the ravages of change—for that peace and serenity which comes only when we have found some permanent, immutable, and eternal values in which to rest. In his cantos on Mutability, possibly the last poetry he wrote, he says that this continual change

> makes me loath this state of life so fickle,
> And love of things so vain to cast away;
> Whose flowering pride, so fading and so fickle,
> Short Time shall soon cut down with his consuming sickle.

Mutability, he says, has not only broken the Laws of Nature but of Justice also, and made wrong of right and bad of good. Spenser sought spiritual strength in thinking of

> that time when no more Change shall be,
> But steadfast rest of all things firmly stayed
> Upon the pillars of Eternity,
> That is contrair to Mutability.

He was a Christian Platonist, and as a Platonist he took a sober view of the place of man in an unfriendly universe, in the midst of forces some of which he must never become reconciled to. Against them he must guard from corruption his most cherished possessions; for corruption ever threatens

> through the rust of time,
> That doth all fairest things on earth deface.

Shakespeare can hardly be called a Christian Platonist, but he was nevertheless as deeply impressed as Spenser with the ravages of Time. If there is any general impression to be derived from the totality of his work, it is that the goodness of life may so easily be lost irretrievably. Time, which changes all, is an enemy of man. It is almost with a sense of shock that we peruse his sonnets and discover how with a kind of noble anger he offers resistance to Time as a bitter foe. He honored Time with a copious vocabulary of denunciation: "this bloody Tyrant," "devouring Time," "Time's fell hand," "Time's tyranny," "Time's fickle glass." He observed that "wasteful Time debateth with decay"; like Diderot he thought it worth noting that

> rocks impregnable are not so stout,
> Nor gates of steel so strong, but Time decays.

But unlike Diderot he hurls back a defiant challenge:

> No, Time, thou shalt not boast that I do change.

In the famous 116th sonnet we get a note of triumph
over Change and Time:

> love is not love
> Which alters when it alteration finds. . . .
> Love's not Time's fool though rosy lips and cheeks
> Within his bending sickle's compass come;
> Love alters not with his brief hours and weeks,
> But bears it out even to the edge of doom.

Going back to the Renaissance in this way, with Spenser
and Shakespeare as representative of it, we can realize
how profoundly the modern world has for two or three
centuries gradually accepted mutability as an axiomatic principle, and used it, not only to describe the
phenomena of the physical world, but to erect a sort
of norm or commandment in the regulation of human
society and in the search for individual salvation and
happiness. Lessing in the eighteenth century declared
that if God offered him the choice between the eternal
possession of truth and the eternal search after truth,
he would choose eternal search, for, he said, it is by
constant search and effort that man increases and per-
fects his energy. The modern world agrees with this
preference and pronounces the conclusion of Dante's
*Paradiso* a bore. Growth, as John Dewey thought, is
the ultimate value. One may question whether those
who choose the eternal search after truth have any but

vague ideas about the duration of eternity, whether
they are going to be happy eternally with frustration.
But for a few years the experience is no doubt exciting,
and it may be plausibly defended as Following Nature.

 *V. PROSPECTS OF UTOPIA*

A careful examination of our United States dollar bill
will discover a Latin phrase on it: *novus ordo seclorum.*
This Latin is an adaptation from the fourth *Eclogue* of
Virgil. In that poem Virgil was celebrating the birth
of a boy—just whom is not known, though in the Middle Ages it was believed that the poet had in this instance been given prophetic powers and that he had
been permitted to announce the coming of the Messiah.
This misinterpretation is explained by the fact that
Virgil plainly did predict a great new Golden Age
under the Emperor Augustus: hence the resonant line
in the poem:

> Magnus ab integro saeclorum nascitur ordo,

which may be rendered into English loosely by Shakespeare's "O brave new world!" or more accurately by
another sonorous line from Shelley's poetic drama
*Hellas* (1821):

> The world's great age begins anew,
>     The golden years return,
> The earth doth like a snake renew
>     Her winter weeds outworn;
> Heaven smiles, and faiths and empires gleam,
> Like wrecks of a dissolving dream. . . .

Another Athens shall arise,
    And to remoter time
Bequeath, like sunset to the skies,
    The splendor of its prime;
And leave, if nought so bright may live,
All earth can take or Heaven can give.

The explanation of the appearance of the Virgilian phrase, *novus ordo seclorum,* on our Great Seal and on our dollar bill is that our nation was formed, as a nation under its own government, at a time when there was a quite general expectation that a great new Golden Age was about to begin. Our Revolution against England was a sign of it, and a few years later the French Revolution, with its dramatic violence and its prophetic program, became an even more startling symbol of the Messianic hopes that inspired the age. Richard Price, a distinguished and able dissenting minister, is perhaps best known because he angered Burke in 1789 by his political sermon on the French Revolution; but Price, like many other people in England at that time, had earlier sympathized with the American Colonies in their struggle for independence, and when the Colonies were victorious in 1781, he preached a sermon on that occasion, taking as his text the Second Epistle of Peter, 3:13: "Nevertheless we, according to his promise, look for new heavens and a new earth, wherein dwelleth righteousness." The young poet Wordsworth, when he visited France in 1791, expected the French Revolution to inaugurate a new age, and therefore he thought that

> Bliss was it in that dawn to be alive,
> But to be young was very heaven.

Looking back to this moment in later years, Wordsworth wrote in his *Prelude:*

> Europe at that time was thrilled with joy,
> France standing on the top of golden hours,
> And human nature seeming born again.

However, the American and French Revolutions were not thought of as the *causes* of the approaching New Age, but rather as good omens, as signs that the New Age was even nearer than might have been supposed. For the whole theory of the future Golden Age had been completely formulated before either Revolution. For instance, Joseph Priestley, the discoverer of oxygen, a prolific writer on philosophy as well as on science, expressed his faith in 1768, eight years before the Declaration of Independence:

> Whatever was the beginning of the world, the end will be glorious and paradisiacal beyond what our imaginations can now conceive. Extravagant as some people may suppose these views to be, I think I could show them to be fairly suggested by the true theory of human nature and to arise from the natural course of human affairs.[1]

Priestley, we observe, states what the basis is for the confident expectation of the millennium, the New Jerusalem, as it was sometimes called; this basis was the new philosophy, the new and true theory of human nature, as Priestley would have it; or as Wordsworth expressed it, human nature seemed to be born again.

We should all be aware of how deeply ingrained this eighteenth-century theory has become in the modern mind. In 1921 James Harvey Robinson, a notable professor of history, published a book called *The Mind in the Making*, which was popular reading at the time and which has been much excerpted for readings for college freshmen ever since. Robinson, with the air of one who was proclaiming a new gospel to the world, urged that we should bring to the moral and social sciences the same scientific method and objectivity and openness of mind that had achieved such obvious success in the physical sciences. Everyone could see that these had been astonishingly effective in adding to our knowledge of the universe. "But the knowledge of man, of the springs of his conduct, of his relation to his fellow-men singly or in groups, and the felicitous regulation of human intercourse in the interest of harmony and fairness, have made no such advance. Aristotle's treatises on astronomy and physics, and his notions . . . of chemical processes, have long gone by the board, but his politics and ethics are still revered. Does this mean that his penetration in the sciences of man exceeded so greatly his grasp of natural science, or does it mean that the progress of mankind in the scientific knowledge and regulation of human affairs has remained almost stationary for over two thousand years? I think we may safely conclude that the latter is the case." Robinson cautiously disclaimed the idea that moral and social science could be "exact" to the same degree as mechanics. But the knowledge of human nature has remained stationary for over two thousand years, and only science can ameliorate this situation. A little further on he suggests that we may do wisely to look on all old ideas with suspicion, and the older the idea the more it should be suspect.

This faith in a scientific regulation of human affairs, in a science of human nature which can be genuinely predictive, has become one of the commonplaces of our time, due to a general drift of opinion of which Professor Robinson's book is only one example. It is the faith which inspires a great deal of current research in the social sciences. In spite of repeated failures and futilities, this hope seems to be inextinguishable. The difficulty, so it is explained to us, is that the science of human behavior is still in the stage of development; but, theoretically, when we have studied the whole range of human behavior with scientific thoroughness, we may well expect that we shall be able to predict all contingencies, that we shall solve all major problems by human engineering. It has to be admitted that at the present time absolute certainty is possible, or at least is being attained, only in mathematics, astronomical physics, and in physical sciences. When we move from these to the biological sciences and medicine, and thence to the social sciences, the role of mathematics grows progressively smaller and the possibility of mathematical certainty keeps on diminishing. Critics of "scientism" point to these facts as indicators that human behavior is not amenable to the same scientific processing as a machine and that a truly exact social science must make the initial assumption that human nature is mechanical. The statistical calculation of probabilities is no more infallible than the shrewd judgment of a man of experience.

The philosophers of the eighteenth century developed, from their inheritance of ideas from the seventeenth, what has been called "the Idea of Progress." This idea was new in modern times. From the Greeks down to the Renaissance, the prevailing philosophy of history was either that the world is steadily deteriorating, or that there is at best a cyclical repetition of deterioration and improvement. It was generally agreed that the past history of mankind was rather disillusioning. But with the seventeenth century, with the stimulus of the new science, men began to turn their eyes more to the promise of the future, and the idea of progress was a philosophy of future history, of a future which would be almost the exact opposite of the miserable past, because man was henceforth to control his own destiny by means of science. Science held out this hope, not just because it provided mankind with new instruments of navigation, or improvements in agriculture or cattle-breeding or cotton-spinning, or with its many other contributions to comfort and ease and the reduction of physical labor. Such practical applications of science give us, when all is said, only a moderate optimism. The new glorious hope of progress was the expectation that science was to be applied, not only to the *tools* that man uses, but to man himself. Let us look again at what Priestley wrote in 1768:

Whatever was the beginning of the world, the end will be glorious and paradisiacal, beyond what our imaginations can now conceive. Extravagant as some may suppose these views to be, I think I could show them to be fairly suggested by the true theory of human nature, and to arise from the natural course of human affairs.

Let us observe especially Priestley's emphasis on the true theory of human nature as fundamental to this optimism. What science offered as its greatest contribution to the life of man was that it would at last give man a true theory of his own nature and thus enable him to control his own destiny. That was the idea of progress. But that is also just what such moderns as James Harvey Robinson and H. G. Wells were offering to the early twentieth century; this modern gospel, which is preached to us every day as something new, was already lifting up the hearts of men two or three centuries ago.

This new and true theory of human nature we have already traced from its formative principles. We have seen that the philosophers were guided and inspired by two great philosophical revelations of the seventeenth century, the science of Newton and the psychology of Locke. From science they learned about the mechanical nature of the universe, from which they deduced that man must also be a mechanism and that the phenomena of man's consciousness must be ex-

plained in terms of cause and effect as rigidly as the
phenomena of the physical world. If we are to make
progress we must apply the same mode of scientific
reasoning both to the physical nature of man and to
his moral and intellectual nature. And from John
Locke they learned that there is nothing in the mind of
man that has not come into it through the senses. These
sensations, they explained, are built up into larger
units in the mind, but no matter how complex our men-
tal operations may become, they are merely the various
combinations of sensations; we cannot jump out of our
psychological skins. What we are is the sum total of
what our experience has made us. We are the products
of our environment and our education. Thus we arrive
by a logical series of propositions at two complemen-
tary conclusions: first, the evil that we currently find
in man is not natural to him; it has been forced into
him by bad education, bad experience, vicious institutions, and old prejudices handed down unintelligently
from generation to generation; secondly, man may be
born again, as Wordsworth put it, by a thorough house
cleaning, by which all this rubbish out of the past is
discarded forever, and a completely new society is
established by reason on the basis of a sound theory
of human nature. Again we observe how science and
sentimentalism combine to lay out a program for Following Nature. Nature, said William Godwin, never
made a dunce. Man, said Helvetius before Godwin, is
born ignorant, but he is not born a sot, and it requires
labor to make him one: "Art and method are necessary;

instruction must heap error upon error; he must have his prejudices multiplied by a multitude of lectures. If sottism be the common condition of mankind among the polished nations, it is the effect of a contagious instruction; it is because they are educated by men of false science, and read sottish books." [2] Education, Helvetius contended, can accomplish everything, both good and evil:

The strongest proof of the power of education is the proportion constantly observed between the diversity of instruction, and its different products or results. . . . If we ask what is the cause that so little just judgment is to be found among the theologians? The duplicity common to them in general results from their education; they are in this respect more assiduously instructed than other men; being accustomed from their youth to content themselves with the jargon of the schools, and to take words for things, it becomes impossible for them to distinguish truth from falsehood, or sophism from demonstration. . . . The soldier is commonly in his youth ignorant and licentious. Why? Because he has no need of instruction. In his later years he is frequently a sot and a fanatic. Why? Because the days of debauchery being then past, his ignorance tends to make him superstitious. . . . Education makes us what we are. . . . The science of education may be reduced perhaps to the placing a man in that situation which will force him to attain the talents and virtues required of him.[3]

The problem of educating the individual is apparently to disappear if we can achieve a reformation of society. Education, we are often told, is coextensive with life—in fact, all life is education. And as education is such a totality of a man's experience, then his environment—

the society and government which control him—is a major part of his education. All this may be granted. But the crux of the argument comes when Helvetius insists that all experience is a one-way affair, the effect of external influences on man. The moral education of the individual is purely and simply the management of his environment, just as Rousseau explained in *Emile*. Helvetius expected government to perform this task in the regeneration of mankind. "Every important reformation in the moral part of education must presuppose a reformation in the laws and form of government." It might seem that such a requirement would offer little hope to a philosopher in France in 1760, the France of Louis XV. But not so. Only continue to sow the seeds of truth in good minds and wait for a favorable time for them to spring up. "The philosopher therefore perceives," said Helvetius, "at a greater or less distance, the time when power will adopt the plan of instruction presented by wisdom; and let him [the philosopher], animated by this hope, endeavour in the meantime to undermine those prejudices that oppose the execution of his plan." [4]

In all of these utterances Helvetius fairly represents the philosophical movement of his time, both in France and England. He explains why the new and true theory of human nature led to such extraordinary optimism, and how it could be possible to speak of human nature being born again. Change the environment in which children grow up, and in a generation or two all the evils will wither and blow away. Let but reason prevail.

Adopt the new ideas propounded by the scientific moralist, the scientific psychologist, the scientific economist and political philosopher, and man will discover that he has unlimited power to change and direct his destiny—nay, even that his nature may become completely perfected. Such was the theory of Progress as it was formulated in the eighteenth century. Such was the theory that nourished the great hope of a new age, a new series of centuries, a Golden Age in the not distant future.

A complete account of the rise and development of the Idea of Progress would be a history of a very large part of the thought of two centuries; a full account of its diffusion into the public mind would lead us into popular literature, into an examination of novels, essays, poetry, and general publications of all kinds. It would lead beyond France and England to Germany, where Herder explained Progress as the cosmic plan of Creative Wisdom which would permit no development to be futile; all God's means are ends, and all His ends are means to higher ends. Humanity therefore moves, in a somewhat fatalistic way, toward its highest goal in the future. In his *Ideas of the Philosophy of the History of Humanity,* begun in 1784, he voiced this hope: "The flower of humanity, captive still in its germ, will blossom out one day into the true form of man like unto God, in a state of which no terrestrial man can imagine the greatness and the Majesty." In the same year Immanuel Kant published a short sketch on the *Idea of a Universal History on a Cosmopolitan*

*Plan,* in which he tried to show how man can progress toward a perfect civil society in the future. Such a cosmopolitan history, he thought, would open up "a consolatory prospect into futurity, in which at a remote distance we shall discover the human species seated upon an eminence won by infinite toil, where all the germs are unfolded which nature has implanted and its own destination upon this earth accomplished." [5] Even the sober and severe Kant cherished the idea of the Millennium, although he believed it could be realized only in the remote future and only after infinite toil.

The most heroic prophet of Progress was the Frenchman Condorcet. He was born in 1743, and was only a young man when the Parisian philosophers were most active. He lived to see the French Revolution, whereas Rousseau and Diderot and Holbach and Helvetius and their friends did not. He took part in the Revolution. But, as we know, each group in power in the French Revolution was soon swept out by a new group which sent its predecessors to the guillotine. Condorcet was among those swept out of power by Robespierre, and he was guillotined in 1794. While he was in hiding, with a fairly certain expectation that he would be discovered and executed, he wrote his prophetic treatise, a *Sketch of a Historical Picture of the Progress of the Human Mind,* which was published the year after his death. In this sketch he distinguished ten periods or stages in the history of man, nine of which were in the past or present, and the tenth in the future. This future period, the period of man made perfect, living in a perfect society, is guaranteed to us by the progress of the human mind, which, as the title indicates, is to be the real source of progress. Thus Condorcet, condemned to death and hiding from an almost certain fate, sat writing his essay in complete confidence in his vision of the perfect human race of the future. This vision, he said, the vision of posterity

freed from its chains, . . . marching with sure steps on the road to virtue, truth, and happiness, consoles the philosopher for the errors, the crimes, the injustices that still soil the earth, and of which he himself is often the victim. It is in the contemplation of this picture . . . that he finds his true recompense for virtue. The contemplation of this picture is an asylum in which the memory of his persecutors does not follow him, an asylum in which, living in imagination with mankind re-established in its rights and in its true nature, he can forget mankind corrupted and tormented by greed, fear, envy. It is in this asylum that he truly lives with his fellows, in a heaven which his reason has created, and which his love of humanity embellishes with the purest joys.[6]

It is not wise to look with too much contempt at these eighteenth-century paeans of jubilation over the approaching Millennium. Some of the doctrines on which they were based have a familar sound even in the mid-twentieth century. First of all, we may note the rejection of history, of the inheritance from the past. History has written the slate full, but full of error, misery, vice. Let us wipe the slate clean and begin all over again. Let us not be weighed down by the dead hand of the past. And as for the institutions and customs which we have inherited from the past, one glance at what they have done to corrupt human nature should be sufficient to condemn them. Men are unfortunately not what they by nature are meant to be, but what society has made them. As Holcroft, the English dramatist and novelist and friend of Godwin, explained: "The generous feelings and higher propensities of the soul are, as it were shrunk up, scarred, violently wrenched, and amputated, to fit us for our intercourse with the world" —the world that past history has made for us. Our efforts to improve human life must therefore be directed, in the first instance, not at any supposed evil within human nature, but at the evil in the environment. Men are now vicious because they are in a way imprisoned in their heritage from the past; liberate them, and their viciousness will depart from them. For all the philosophers with the single exception of Helvetius were convinced that man is naturally good. They were convinced that he can become good and even reach a state of perfection because by changing human institutions human nature itself will be born again. Those who should manage human affairs, the scientific moralists and law-givers, the educators, the statesmen, are all, as Holbach stated it, "gardeners who can by varying systems of cultivation alter the character of men as they would alter the form of trees." All this moral and political geometry is spun out by the overruling reason, which makes its prescriptions for a simplified and abstract Man, for man as he must be assumed to be if science is to understand and explain him completely.[7]

Are such ideas and such reasonings still current among us? Some unquestionable authorities have thought so. A revealing remark was once made by A.D. Lindsay, master of Balliol College at Oxford, and distinguished not only as a Greek scholar but also as a Socialist and leader of the Labor Party in England. In 1928 he contributed a brief preface to the English translation of Elie Halévy's study of *The Growth of Philosophic Radicalism*. He thought that it is of "special interest and value to us at present" to see Halévy's "convincing demonstration of how deeply the Benthamites were influenced by their belief in the possibilities of applying to the study of man and society the principles and methods of the physical sciences. This is the clue to some of the most curious aberrations of their thought, and to much of their short-sightedness. The belief is still with us. It is curious how often men are still found to argue, in the manner of Bentham, that if certain things are admitted to be true, sociology could not be an exact science, and therefore the admissions must not be made." He concluded that perhaps "the most striking impression which the book makes is how much of our thought on modern social problems, whether we call ourselves individualists or socialists, still follows the lines laid down by, and still accepts the presuppositions of, the philosophical radicals." On the question of the goodness of human nature Reinhold Niebuhr has remarked that "no cumulation of contradictory evidence seems to disturb modern man's good opinion of himself. He considers himself the victim

of corrupting institutions which he is about to destroy
or reconstruct, or of the confusions of ignorance which
an adequate education is about to overcome. Yet he
continues to regard himself as essentially harmless and
virtuous." Finally, there is testimony from behind the
Iron Curtain that may well give us pause. It comes
from I. K. Luppol, a Moscow philosopher, whose book
on Diderot and his philosophical ideas was translated
into French in 1936. Luppol first speaks for himself:
"Are the morals of a nation bad? The cause is bad
laws, a deplorable form of government. To improve
the manners and morals it is therefore necessary to
change the structure of the state. This is the aspect of
the social doctrine of French materialism which Karl
Marx had in mind when he wrote that eighteenth-century French materialism leads directly to socialism
and communism." Then Luppol quotes Marx as follows: "It does not require much intelligence to grasp
the connection between materialist doctrine on the one
hand, a doctrine which teaches the innate tendency of
man to goodness, the equality of intellectual aptitudes
among all men, the omnipotence of experience, habit,
and education, the influence of external circumstances
on a man's nature, etc., and on the other hand, communism and socialism." [8] Russian theory seems to continue officially faithful to Marx on these matters. Genetics, the study of heredity, contradicts the theory of
the omnipotence of the environment. More than twenty
years ago Moscow decreed that genetics is an antisocial
science and refused to allow the geneticists of the

world to hold their Congress in Russia. The ideas that we find in the musty old books of the eighteenth century have not died away completely; to each new generation the old ideas appear fresh and new.

English disciples of the Parisian philosophers would, however, have shuddered at the thought of finding a communistic state at the end of their speculative course. Lovers of freedom as they were, they preferred as little government as possible, and ideally none at all. The most impressive exponent of this tendency was William Godwin, whose two-volume work on *Political Justice,* published in 1793, fired all the generous youth of England. William Hazlitt wrote a generation later that Godwin "blazed as a sun in the firmament of reputation; no one was more talked of, more looked up to, more sought after, and wherever liberty, truth, justice was the theme, his name was not far off." Coleridge, Wordsworth, and Southey, all of them then young men in their twenties, became his disciples. "Throw away your books on chemistry," Wordsworth counseled a young student of the Temple, "and read Godwin on Necessity." A generation later Shelley became first a convert to Godwin's ideas and then his son-in-law. When we examine the contents of the two volumes we meet again the familiar doctrines of Helvetius and Holbach. Godwin learned them from the French, and he repeats them, the idea of cause and effect governing completely the nature of man, the all-important power of experience in fashioning our minds, and so on. But Godwin differed from the Pari-

sians in important ways; for instance, the French were
inclined to hope that the regeneration of the world
would come about by having the governments adopt
the ideas of the philosophers and putting them in effect; we must remember that this was the era of the
enlightened despots, such as Frederick of Prussia and
the Empress Catherine of Russia, both of whom wished
to be considered admirers of the new philosophers.
But Godwin would have nothing to do with governments. He contended that government is distinct from
society, and he agreed with Paine that "society is produced by our wants, and government by our wicked-
ness." [9] As for progress in the discovery and dissemination of truth, government could only be a hindrance;
by its very nature it is repressive and hostile to the improvements of the individual mind. The intellectual
salvation of man is possible only as we move in the
direction of a state of near anarchy. In his two volumes
Godwin found room to canvass the whole range of institutions and demonstrate the necessity of abolishing
all of them: monarchy, of course, but also all other
forms of government, aristocracy, the church—not
only state churches, but all of them—private property,
marriage, the principle of majority rule, all coercive
law and all law courts, and even juries, except as they
might operate in a purely advisory capacity. The ideal
society would be one in which man is uninhibited by
any external compulsion, but whose whole life is the
free and spontaneous fulfillment of his natural social
inclinations, enlightened and guided by reason.

Reason is probably the key concept of his philosophy. Godwin wanted a revolution, but he wanted nothing by force, not even the triumph of truth. It was clear to Godwin that the revolution that was needed could and should come about by the prevalence of sheer reason, by the dissemination of truth from one convert to another. According to the law of cause and effect, it is impossible for the mind, once it has apprehended truth, to resist the effect of it, for man, said Godwin, is by definition a rational being. "If there be any man who is incapable of making inferences for himself, or of understanding, when stated in the most explicit terms, the inferences of another, him we consider as an abortive production, and not in strictness belonging to the human species." [10] In view of the many readers of Godwin who could not agree with him, it would seem rather harsh for Godwin to define them as abortive productions and not in strictness belonging to the human species. It is evident, we read, that if those into whose hands the sacred cause of truth may be intrusted will do justice to its merits, then truth "includes in it the indestructible germ of ultimate victory. Every new convert that is made to its cause, if he is taught its excellence as well as its reality, is a fresh apostle to extend its illumination through a wider sphere. In this respect it resembles the motion of a falling body, which increases its rapidity in proportion to the squares of the distances." [11] No one can doubt that truth is mighty and will prevail by its own irresistible force if it is governed by such a mathematical law in its operation, a law analogous to the law of gravitation. But it seems clear that Godwin did not arrive at this conclusion by experience, but by pure geometrical reasoning from a priori definitions.

From this doctrine of the omnipotence of truth there follows that the lives of men must necessarily be changed as truth is disseminated in ever wider circles. For Godwin was able to demonstrate also that our actions are governed absolutely by our reason. "Whatever is brought home to the understanding, so long as it is present to the mind, possesses an undisputed empire over the conduct." The moral weaknesses and vices of men are therefore not invincible. For these "are founded upon ignorance and error; but truth is more powerful than any champion that can be brought into the field against it; consequently truth has the faculty of expelling weakness and vice, and placing nobler and more beneficent principles in their stead." [12] Man is, therefore, a perfectible being and the instrument of his perfection is the force of omnipotent reason. But we have yet to explore what kind of being man will be when he becomes perfected. What does Godwin mean by Justice? And what kind of virtue will be practiced by the perfected man? Here Godwin parts company with Helvetius, who held the Hobbesian doctrine of the natural selfishness of human nature, and expected the government to unite all the many individual selfish interests into one harmonious mutual good. But Godwin, like Diderot and Rousseau and most of the philosophers, believed in the natural goodness of human nature, and like most of them, he held that the prime and all-embracing virtue, the one virtue from which all other goodness could emanate, is benevolence. By the time of Godwin the Utilitarians had evolved a formula for guiding this benevolence: the greatest good of the greatest number—good being usually understood as the equivalent of happiness, and happiness as the presence of pleasure and the absence of pain. Bentham had already worked out a calculus of moral values on this basis, a calculus of pleasures and pains. Godwin derived his theory of virtue both from this sentimental doctrine of benevolence and from the Utilitarian theory of the greater benefit to the whole. Virtue is therefore the desire of the happiness of the human species; but a virtuous act must also be the result of the knowledge of some truth, and this truth must be a reasoned calculation that a certain act will conduce to the happiness of the species. Virtue is thus the necessary consequence of holding the right ideas and making the right calculations. "Where it exists in any eminence," said Godwin, "it is a species of conduct, modelled upon a true estimate of the different reasons inviting us to preference." [13] Accordingly the Golden Rule falls a little short; it does not require the exercise of the calculating reason: "This maxim, though possessing considerable merit as a popular principle, is not modelled with the strictness of philosophical accuracy." [14]

Unfortunately, things being as they are, we must, most of us, undergo a kind of purging before we can live on this high level of rationality. We are all vitiated by our institutions, our customs, and our inherited prejudices, and we must free ourselves from these trammels which continually hinder the reason. Godwin thought up a situation which would drive home the lesson that we must ever keep in mind—the greater good of the greater number. It happened that Godwin admired Archbishop Fénelon for his widely read philosophical narrative *Telemachus* and believed that by writing this book Fénelon had indisputably done a great good to a great number. Suppose, then, that you were to find the house of the Archbishop in flames and that you had to choose whether to rescue the author writing his book or his chambermaid. Which should you choose? Not the chambermaid, as irrational chivalrous tradition would dictate; for there are few of us "that would hesitate to pronounce" that the prelate with the unfinished masterpiece would contribute more to the happiness, information, and improvement of others than a mere chambermaid. But Godwin presses on to expose some even more insidious considerations. Suppose, he goes on, that the chambermaid were your wife, or your mother; according to rational calculation, "this would not alter the truth of the proposition." The choice of the more valuable life is what Godwin calls justice, and mere gratitude or affection would merely confuse the issue. These remarks caused some scandal at the time, and in the third edition of his work Godwin altered the chambermaid to a valet and the wife or mother to father or brother. But the objection remained that family feeling and gratitude are irrelevant in questions of justice and virtue.[15]

If we follow such a rule of reason, we will make no promises of any kind. Promises are always immoral. What we promise must be either right or wrong. If it is right, we will do what we promise by the immutable laws of reason and the promise is unnecessary. If it is wrong, the promise violates the principle of justice and is obviously immoral. Marriage vows are examples of such irrationality, and so also are treaties between nations.

But of all the evils to be abolished by the omnipotence of reason, the greatest in Godwin's estimation was property. "With grief it must be confessed," he says, "that, however great and excessive are the evils that are produced by monarchies and courts, by the imposture of priests and the iniquity of criminal laws, all these are imbecile and impotent compared with the evils that arise out of the established system of property." [16] The evil lies in the concept that something is mine; for the idea of anything being personal and private naturally contradicts the principle that we must always first consider the general good. What I have does not belong to me; I hold it in trust for others; if they need it more than I do, it belongs to them. "My neighbor is in want of ten pounds that I can spare. . . . Unless it can be shown that the money can be more beneficently employed, his right is as complete as if he had my bond in his possession, or had supplied me with goods to the amount." [17] That is, property belongs, not necessarily to him who has worked for it, but to him who needs it most. Would such a practice lead to interminable squabbles between neighbors? Not in an ideal society. "In a state of society where men lived in the midst of plenty, and where all shared alike in the bounties of nature, these sentiments [envy, malice, revenge, the spirit of oppression, the spirit of fraud] would inevitably expire. The narrow principle of selfishness would vanish. No man being obliged to guard his little store, or provide, with anxiety and pain, for his restless wants, each would lose his individual existence in the thought of the general good. No man would be an enemy to his neighbor, for they would have no subject of contention; and of consequence, philanthropy would resume the empire which reason assigns her." [18]

It is difficult to imagine how philanthropy could be the general activity in a society in which no one has any property and no one has any wants. But here we have reached Godwin's idea of justice; it is that in a society animated by benevolence and governed by reason, every man will have what he needs and every other man will gladly give it to him. Who is to decide what he needs? Unerring reason will resolve all such questions, and perfected man will obey reason. As Hazlitt said about Bentham, "Strict logicians are licensed visionaries."

As human nature and society approach this state of perfection, institution after institution will become useless and disappear. Godwin conceded that it may be necessary at some points in this transition to use a little authority and violence, but not much, and even this necessity "does not appear to arise out of the nature of man, but out of the institutions by which he has been corrupted. Man is not originally vicious. . . . Render the plain dictates of justice level to every capacity . . . and the whole species will become reasonable and virtuous." [19] In that condition juries, for instance, will cease to render verdicts; it will be sufficient for them to make recommendations; nay, why should twelve men be used when the reason of one man can perform the task as well as the identical reasons of twelve? And why should there be elections? Will not the competence of one individual to instruct his neighbors be a matter of sufficient notoriety, without the formality of an election? And so on. Even philosophic reason could set no limits to the glorious prospects that might lie ahead. Godwin, for his part, hoped that in this bright future medicine would conquer not only disease but death. With the complete supremacy of reason, and with the world well populated and no one dying, the propagation of children can be dispensed with. "The whole will then be a people of men, and not of children. Generation will not succeed generation, nor truth have in a certain degree to recommence her career every thirty years. Other improvements may be expected to keep pace with those of health and longevity. There will be no war, no crimes, no administration of justice as it is called, and no government. Beside this, there will be neither disease, anguish, melancholy, nor resentment. Every man will seek, with ineffable ardor, the good of all." [20]

Such was Godwin's dream for the future in 1793. Such was the dream that captivated the best youth of that turbulent decade. The world's great age was to begin anew, and human nature was to be born again. Unfortunately, the French Revolution soon belied its promise and developed into the Reign of Terror, and shortly thereafter Napoleon appeared, the man on horseback. Instead of Utopia, England and Europe were to experience a whole generation of war and hardship. When Shelley appeared, after it was all over, and began the concluding chorus of his poetic drama *Hellas* with the swelling and hopeful strain,

> The world's great age begins anew,
> The golden years return,

he concluded the last stanza with lament and disillusionment,

> Drain not to its dregs the urn
>   Of bitter prophecy.
> The world is weary of the past,
>   Oh, might it die or rest at last!

There were those in the eighteenth century who foresaw this line of development. They objected that the revolutionary thought was inadequate in its fundamental assumptions, that its method was unsound, and that it was devoid of practical wisdom. The greatest of these critics was Edmund Burke.

## VI. BURKE AND THE RECONSTRUCTION OF SOCIAL PHILOSOPHY

During his lifetime Burke was perhaps best known as a politician who, as his friend Goldsmith wrote, in an inverted compliment, "to party gave up what was meant for mankind." But after his death it was soon recognized that Burke had in fact given to mankind a great and profound philosophy of society and government. In his youth Coleridge had been an enthusiastic disciple of Godwin and in a sonnet in 1794 accused Burke of having "with wizard spell blasted the laurelled fame of Freedom"; but some twenty years later, in his *Biographia Literaria,* he could praise Burke as a political seer, who referred habitually to principles. "In Burke's writings, indeed, the germs of almost all political truths may be found." These principles governed the opinions of Burke throughout his career. "Let the scholar who doubts this assertion refer only to the speeches and writings of Edmund Burke at the commencement of the American War and compare them with his speeches and writings at the commencement of the French Revolution. He will find the principles exactly the same and the deductions the same." In the Victorian era John Morley, who was not without sympathy for the revolutionary philosophers of the eighteenth century, contributed his own famous trib-

ute. In his admirable little biography of Burke he
praised the speeches on the struggle with the American
Colonies: "It is no exaggeration to say that they compose the most perfect manual in our literature or in
any literature, for one who approaches the study of
public affairs, whether for knowledge or for practice.
They are an example without fault of all the qualities
which the critic, whether a theorist or an actor, of great
political situations should strive by night and by day
to possess."

Notwithstanding this great reputation and authority
as a political thinker, Burke was not a philosopher, but
a statesman. He himself once happened to distinguish
between the two: "A statesman differs from a professor
in an university: the latter has only the general view of
society; the former, the statesman, has a number of
circumstances to combine with those general ideas, and
to take into his consideration." It is a striking and
significant fact that the speculative revolutionary
thinkers wrote in the retirement of the study, whereas
Burke's writings are all speeches and pamphlets, the
products of thirty years in the House of Commons.
They are all utterances on specific issues before the
House and the nation, all of them realistic discussions
of actual current problems. And almost all of his par-
liamentary life was spent in the opposition, championing causes which, for the moment at least, went down to
defeat. He was always an active fighter in the thick of
battle. He wrote no treatise on the evil of slavery, but
he drew up a specific plan for stopping the worst evils

of the institution and for gradually abolishing it in an orderly manner; it was not adopted in his lifetime. He fought for greater economic freedom for Ireland, but without much success. He tried to give the Roman Catholics in England and Ireland some relief from the oppressive penal laws under which they still suffered, but real relief came to them only after Burke had passed away. He opposed those policies of George III and his ministries which drove the American Colonies to rebellion and secession, but all his efforts were in vain. He led in the attack of the House of Commons on Warren Hastings and the misgovernment of the natives of India, and here he had some success in forcing improvement in the India policy, even though Hastings was acquitted in the trial before the House of Lords. Such is the record of Burke's activities in the House of Commons—ever fighting, ever in the opposition to the ministry and the policies that were victorious, ever championing the cause of the oppressed.

But when the French Revolution broke out in 1789, Burke attacked it in his *Reflections,* undoubtedly one of the greatest and most influential political pamphlets of all time. Burke's critics and enemies have accused him of thus stirring up all Europe into an unfortunate reaction against the Revolution. Many agreed with Coleridge that he had blasted the laureled fame of Freedom. Why did Burke, the champion of the oppressed, so suddenly turn all his power of denunciation and invective against this uprising of the oppressed French? Morley has said the last and decisive word on this apparent inconsistency: Burke changed his front, but he never changed his ground. As Coleridge said, Burke's principles remained exactly the same and his deductions the same. It was the principles operative in the French Revolution that Burke most feared, and against them he was forced into adamantine opposition by those principles which he had himself cherished all his life. He thought that the French Revolution, under the leaders it had and in the course it took, was far more than a struggle for economic improvement or political reform. In the *Reflections* (1790) he declared that the most important of all revolutions that may be dated from the sixth of October, 1789, was "a revolution in sentiments, manners, and moral opinions." In his *Thoughts on French Affairs*, written in 1791, he observed that this Revolution is unlike any previous political revolution in the history of Europe: "It is a Revolution of doctrine and theoretic dogma." In his *Letter to a Noble Lord* (1796) he calls it "a subject of awful meditation. Before this of France, the annals of all time have not furnished an instance of a *complete* revolution. That Revolution seems to have extended even to the constitution of the mind of man." In his *Second Letter on a Regicide Peace* (1796) he asserted that "a silent revolution in the moral world preceded the political, and prepared it." Burke's attacks on the French Revolution were a continuous battle for the minds of men.

Accordingly, Burke in one place or another objected to almost every step in the dialectic of the speculative philosophies of the Revolution. He objected to their basic fondness for a mathematical type of reasoning in politics. But this was an objection he had already voiced in 1775 in his speech *On Conciliation:* "Aristotle, the great master of reasoning, cautions us, and with great weight and propriety, against this species of delusive geometrical accuracy in moral arguments, as the most fallacious of all sophistry." He returns to it in the *Reflections* (1790): "Political reasoning is a computing principle: adding, subtracting, multiplying, and dividing, morally, and not metaphysically or mathematically, true moral denominations." And in the *Appeal from the New to the Old Whigs* (1791) he declared that "pure metaphysical abstraction does not belong to these matters. The lines of morality are not like the ideal lines of mathematics. They are broad and deep as well as long. They admit of exceptions; they demand modifications. These exceptions and modifications are not made by the process of logic, but by the rules of prudence." Prudence is a concept not highly valued either in logic or in mathematics. Once it is admitted into political philosophy as a virtue, it brings with it a wholly different conception of the nature of man and of society.

Instead of Godwin's man, "screwed up by mood and figure into a logical machine," as Hazlitt said, Burke presents a conception of a nature infinitely complex and even paradoxical. Man, he said, is at once a most wise and a most unwise being. In the *Reflections* he insisted that we need artificial institutions "to fortify

the fallible and feeble contrivances of our reason."
In a famous passage he described that purging of human nature which was the program of the Revolutionists: "All the pleasing illusions, which made power
gentle and obedience liberal, which harmonized the
different shades of life, and which, by a bland assimila-
tion incorporated into politics the sentiments which
beautify and soften private society, are to be dissolved
by this new conquering empire of light and reason. All
the decent drapery of life is to be rudely torn off. All
the superadded ideas, furnished from the wardrobe of
a moral imagination, which the heart owns and the
understanding ratifies as necessary to cover the defects
of our naked, shivering human nature, and to raise it
to dignity in our own estimation, are to be exploded
as ridiculous, absurd, and antiquated fashion." Burke
saw many needs of human nature not visible to Godwin, who, as if to justify every phrase of Burke's con-
demnation, published *Political Justice* three years
later. Of no group of men in the history of thought
could one say more truly than of these revolutionary
speculators what John Adams said of man in general,
that he is a reasoning, but not a reasonable, animal.
Godwin was not aware that feeble contrivances were
possible to the human reason; and as Hazlitt has said,
he absolves man from all ties of attachment to individuals so that he may devote himself to the pursuit of
universal benevolence.

No *philosophe* ever meditated on the needs of our
naked and shivering human nature. There was to be no

chill in the moral weather of Utopia. But Burke could consider what was necessary to raise human nature to dignity in our own estimation. Burke was no Calvinist and did not say much about the depravity of the human species; quite the contrary, he who despises man, he said, despises God. But neither did he have such confidence in the natural goodness and capacity of man that he would trust each man's conduct to his own judgment or inclination. It is not only sheer foolish pride of intellect, it is a perversion of the intellect, a kind of metaphysical madness, for any man of speculation to sit down and write in a book the details of a completely new form of society. "We, in England," he retorted to his French correspondent, "are afraid to put men to live and trade each on his own private stock of reason; because we suspect that this stock in each man is small, and that the individuals would do better to avail themselves of the general bank and capital of nations and ages." He even took issue with the thinkers of France in the matter of prejudices, which they were constantly combating as the source of the worst evils; he suggested to them that instead of trying to explode old prejudices, they would do well to employ their sagacity to discover what latent wisdom might be in them. Good prejudices are valuable; they render "a man's virtue his habit, and not a series of unconnected acts. Through just prejudice a man's duty becomes a part of his nature."

Coleridge accused Burke of deserting the cause of liberty, and so, evidently, did Burke's French friend,

Monsieur Dupont. In October, 1789, Burke replied to him: "You hope, sir, that I think the French deserving of liberty. I certainly do. I certainly think that all men who desire it, deserve it. It is not the reward of our merit, or the acquisition of our industry. It is our inheritance. It is the birthright of our species. . . . But the liberty I mean is a *social* freedom. It is that state of things in which liberty is secured by the equality of restraint. . . . This kind of liberty is, indeed, but another name for justice; ascertained by wise laws, and secured by well-constructed institutions. . . . But whenever a separation is made between liberty and justice, neither is, in my opinion, safe." But fifteen years before, in a speech to his constituents in Bristol, he had already said that "the liberty, the only liberty, I mean is a liberty connected with order: that not only exists along with order and virtue, but which cannot exist at all without them." In 1780 he again told his constituents that "I have no idea of a liberty unconnected with honesty and justice." In this argument that the liberty that is really valuable to man is a liberty connected with a social order, Burke was again implying a conception of man and society directly opposite to the theories of the Revolution.

Such a social order, the condition of a true and manly freedom, seemed to Burke to be possible of achievement, like the English Constitution, only by the perseverance and effort of many generations, by the concurrence of many men and many tempers and many events, by embodying in institutions the wisdom of a whole people accumulated through many years; but such a social order, he lamented, can be demolished in a moment by the rashness and fury of very ordinary man. And the new revolutionary philosophy was tearing up the whole vast fabric of the social inheritance of Europe, and replacing it with untried innovations. It was this new philosophy which stirred Burke most deeply as he wrote his *Reflections*. He warned that Europe was losing its old glory and its humanity in an age of sophisters, economists, and calculators, whose paper constitutions and speculative novelties were being imposed by force upon a whole nation. But we in England, he wrote to his friend in Paris, have not yet succumbed to the innovations of these philosophers. "We are not the converts of Rousseau; we are not the disciples of Voltaire; Helvetius has made no progress amongst us. . . . We know that *we* have made no discoveries, and we think that no discoveries are to be made, in morality; nor many in the great principles of government, nor in the idea of liberty, which were understood long before we were born, altogether as well as they will be after the grave has heaped its mould upon our presumption, and the silent tomb shall have imposed its law on our pert loquacity." We shall do well to look more carefully at our social inheritance, the world into which we are born, to understand what needs it was intended to meet, and what its meaning is for the life of man.

Politics then, according to Burke, ought to be adjusted, not to bare human reason, but to human nature, of which reason is but a part, and, he adds, by no means the greatest part. Burke could not have conceived of a nation or a people or a community as anything like a collection of machines in a factory, all beautifully adjusted and synchronized by a system of belts and transmissions, regulated by human engineering; neither would he believe that human felicity could be found in any anarchic state of nature. To form a good and humane society, Burke thought, many things are necessary in addition to good laws; he emphasized the importance of religion, traditions of living, a rich heritage of customs, a complex pattern of relationships of all kinds, such as would not only develop the personality of the individual—to use the popular phrase of our day—but which would also teach him the truth about his own nature by their discipline of him. Burke had some insight into social psychology. "A nation," he said, "is a moral essence, not a geographical arrangement." We do not get a *people*, in any significant sense, merely by herding many individuals into one locality. A people, Burke believed, is a moral essence formed under the discipline of nature. "When great multitudes act together, under the discipline of nature, I then recognize the *people*." This nature is of course not the nature under which primitive man was then supposed to live, but the discipline of a complex society. It included even a tradition of manners.

What other political thinker has dwelt on the importance of manners or considered it pertinent to his subject? Yet Burke, on his general principles, could even declare that "manners are of more importance than laws. Upon them, in a great measure, the laws depend. The law touches us but here and there, and now and then. Manners are what vex or soothe, corrupt or purify, exalt or debase, barbarize or refine us, by a constant, steady, uniform, insensible operation, like that of the air we breathe in. They give their whole form and color to our lives. According to their quality, they aid morals, they supply them, or they totally destroy them." But manners are, of course, the product of a disciplining social tradition, of a bringing-up. The unregulated impulses, whether of the child or the adult, do not always lead to good manners; there has to be a firm and sometimes painful exertion of authority, a persevering insistence on right habits, and a vigilant instruction in ideals and right sentiments; and all of these would be included in Burke's concept of the discipline of nature.

Here as everywhere else in Burke's thought, he took his stand in profound opposition to the spirit and the doctrines of the revolutionary philosophers, who were always drawing a distinction between art and nature. The natural is always good, the artificial is always bad. Let the child but be natural; let him follow his own impulses and make his own decisions. Rousseau, who wrote a whole book about the education of one boy, made no provision for the instruction of Emile in manners. And in everything else, as well as in manners,

Rousseau insisted that the natural instincts and impulses must not be perverted by what is artificial—and all civilization had to be proscribed as artificial.

Whether or not we have directly inherited the presumptions of the eighteenth-century philosophers, we moderns are much in the habit of drawing the same distinction between art and nature. When a primitive man in a far-away island makes a hut of branches and thatch, that is natural. When we make a building of stone and concrete and brick, that is artificial. When a primitive man decorates his shield, that is natural; when he dances and chants, that is also natural; but a modern symphony or opera or ballet is the product of civilization and we hesitate to call it natural. We are still in many ways strangely committed to the cult of the primitive. When a scientific anthropologist turns his attention to the problem of what religion is and what it means in the life of man, he goes straight to the uncontaminated tribes of Africa or the remotest islands of the Pacific; I have yet to meet an anthropologist who has turned for help in this problem to the Epistles of Saint Paul or the writings of Saint Augustine. This kind of preference for the primitive as more natural than the products of civilization Burke condemned as a very dangerous misconception. In a pregnant aphorism he demolished the whole theory: art, he said, is man's nature. "Nature," he said in another place, "is never more truly herself than in her grandest forms. The Apollo of Belvedere is as much in nature as any clown by Teniers." Such a statement has immense implications. We must conclude from it that the grand and complex compositions of Bach and Beethoven are as truly natural to man as the chants of aborigines. We must conclude that the highly developed society and government of England or France in the eighteenth century were as natural to man as the comparatively simple life in Tahiti.

As a further consequence we must conclude that society as we find it is a revelation of the real nature of man. The revolutionary philosophers were all in agreement on the proposition that man is naturally good and that all the evil we are suffering is due to bad institutions and conventions. But they never even recognized the problem raised by their proposition; they never tried to explain whence came these evil institutions and conventions. Obviously, they are the constructs of man himself. If they are evil, they are good scientific evidence of some evil within man. If they are good, they bear testimony to something good in man. It must be clear that the nature of man cannot be set in opposition to the artifacts he has made. Burke was never in danger of falling into this error. He was a realist and took human nature as he found it, a mixture of good and bad. Man is weak and naked and unwise; nevertheless he has wisely devised institutions and conventions and social customs whereby he may be clothed, supported, and guided. These are a necessary part of his life; they provide that discipline of nature which sustains his humanity.

It may therefore be said that Burke agreed with the

philosophers in one point, at least, in his belief that
society is a contrivance made by man. But his disagreement with them is more important than this apparent
agreement. It is often said that society is not a machine
but an organism; and there are historians who neatly
contrast Burke with the French philosophers by saying
that the philosophers looked on society as a machine,
whereas Burke thought of it more as an organism. It is
fairly correct to say that the revolutionists believed
that they could simply rebuild the machine according
to scientific specifications and a perfect performance
would be guaranteed. It would also be fair to Burke to
say that he would not have thought that a weak or ailing
member of an organism could be easily replaced by a
new one, a new liver or kidney, for instance, but rather
that the improvement would have to take place in the
liver or kidney one already has, by a judicious regimen
of life and a course of medication.

The theory of the organism is of course the more
modern, held by social thinkers of the nineteenth and
twentieth centuries. But this contrast is not quite the
whole truth about Burke. We say that constitutions are
not made, but grow. Burke said that they are made and
also that they grow. He once remarked that such analo-
gies are dangerous if they are pressed too far. Society
and government are in one respect like a machine in
that they are contrivances of man to meet his needs,
and he can change them if he wants to. The English
Constitution, Burke said, has often been looked into
and modified, and always for the better. Every consti-

tution, he insisted, must have in it a provision for change and amendment, because this is the indispensable means of its preservation and continuance. Burke repeated again and again that government is a human contrivance. But he also said that art is man's nature, that human contrivances are like the human beings that contrive them, that a commonwealth is a moral essence, and that we shall be quite inadequate in our contriving if we ignore the difference between a machine and human nature. It is not the whole truth to say with Locke that our minds are at birth like clean slates; we are born with all sorts of individual tendencies and weaknesses and aptitudes which may develop only slowly through the years, and each individual has to work through life with what he was born with; he cannot be sent back to the factory for overhauling. And so also with society and government; it is a human contrivance, but it is strangely more than that; for if we pursue the inquiry into the nature of society far enough, we are led to see what Burke called a "stupendous wisdom moulding together the great mysterious incorporation of the human race."

When modern commentators come to this aspect of Burke's thought, they usually drop the subject rather hastily and murmur something about the deep mysticism of Burke's nature. It may be that mysticism should not be admitted into social science. But it would seem strange to exclude from the science of man any recognition of such things as hopes and loyalties and aspirations. It is entirely reasonable to assume that when dealing with such material as human nature we may need insights that are not easily arrived at by the sheer force of reason. Such insights may be necessary to correct the deliverances of strict rationality. It may therefore be profitable to examine a couple of passages from Burke in which he scrutinizes the phraseology and doctrine that almost all advanced thinkers accepted in his time, tests them, and corrects and reinterprets them to give them deeper significance and to make them conform to the realities of our existence.

From the time of Locke down to Burke it was generally thought to be axiomatic that society was formed by a contract entered into with free consent between the members of it, and that when this contract is broken it becomes null and void and each person is restored to the original liberty he enjoyed in the state of nature. All sorts of variations were played on this theme, and the theory of secessionism in our Southern states before the Civil War was one lingering heritage from it. If our relations with our fellow men are a matter of contract, freely and voluntarily entered into, our duties and responsibilities are within our own determination, and we are ourselves the judges as to what circumstances would occasion our giving notice of the termination of the contract. Theoretically, the door is thus left wide open for revolution, and the theory was considered indispensable by the revolutionary leaders of the eighteenth century. But even when the extreme of revolution was impossible of accomplishment, any serious grievances would under the theory raise the question of the legitimacy of government. Thus any agitation for reform would tend to generate turbulence and shake society, not merely physically, but to its moral foundations.

Burke questioned the adequacy of this theory from one point of view by inquiring into the nature of our duties as we encounter them in our daily life. "I cannot too often recommend it to the serious consideration of all men who think civil society to be within the province of moral jurisdiction, that, if we owe it any duty, it is not subject to our will. Duties are not voluntary. Duty and will are even contradictory terms. . . . Look through the whole of life and the whole system of duties. Much the strongest obligations are such as were never the results of our option. . . . We have obligations to mankind at large which are not the consequence of any voluntary pact. They arise from the relation of man to man, and the relation of man to God, which relations are not matters of choice. On the contrary, the force of all the pacts which we enter into with any particular person or number of persons amongst mankind depends upon these prior obligations. In some cases the subordinate relations are voluntary, in others they are necessary, but the duties are all compulsive. When we marry, the choice is voluntary, but the duties are not matter of choice: they are dictated by the nature of the situation. Dark and inscrutable are the ways by which we come into the world. The instincts which give rise to this mysterious process of Nature are not of our making. But out of physical causes, unknown to us, perhaps unknowable, arise moral duties, which, as we are able perfectly to comprehend, we are bound indispensably to perform. Parents may not be consenting to their moral relation; but, consenting or not, they are bound to a long train of burdensome duties towards those with whom they have never made a convention of any sort. Children are not consenting to their relation; but their relation, without their actual consent, binds them to its duties,— or rather it implies their consent, because the presumed consent of every rational creature is in unison with the predisposed order of things. Men come in that manner into a community with the social state of their parents, endowed with all the benefits, loaded with all the duties of their situation." These are the realities of life. In such a simple matter as the reciprocal relationships of parents and children, the contract theory of society becomes, to say the least, impossible. A family is not, any more than a nation, a mere aggregation of individuals. In its multitude of relationships it demands that we perform our duties, it forces us to submit our wills to the discipline of nature, it gives a moral quality to human life.

In another passage Burke transforms the contract theory into nothing less than the ancient doctrine of the Law of Nature. He begins with a seeming concession to the current doctrine. "Society," he said, "is indeed a contract." But if so, what kind of contract? "Subordinate contracts for objects of mere occasional interest may be dissolved at pleasure—but the State ought not to be considered as nothing better than a partnership agreement in a trade of pepper and coffee, calico or tobacco, or some other such low concern, to be taken up for a little temporary interest, and to be dissolved by the fancy of the parties. It is to be looked on with other reverence; because it is not a partnership in things subservient only to the gross animal existence of a temporary and perishable nature. It is a partnership in all science; a partnership in all art; a partnership in every virtue, and in all perfection. As the ends of such a partnership cannot be obtained in many generations, it becomes a partnership not only between those who are living, but between those who are living, those who are dead, and those who are to be born. Each contract of each particular State is but a clause in the great primeval contract of eternal society, linking the lower with the higher natures, connecting the visible and invisible world, according to a fixed compact sanctioned by the inviolable oath which holds all physical and all moral natures each in their appointed place. This law is not subject to the will of those who by an obligation above them, and infinitely superior, are bound to submit their will to that law."

On this passage the late Professor Hearnshaw of the University of London has remarked as follows: "If one asks what is the meaning of this sonorous passage, the answer is that as it stands it has none. It is resounding nonsense . . . What could a sober lawyer make of an agreement between the dead and the unborn; from whom would he get his fee? . . . Language has obviously lost its ordinary meaning." [1] But, curiously, such a criticism could be valid, not against Burke, but rather against the bald theory as Locke left it and as it came to Burke; for that very reason Burke is here transforming the theory. Burke begins with the standard term *contract;* it changes to *agreement,* then to *compact* and partnership, until we reach the great primeval contract of eternal society over which, we may note, there are no lawyers' fees to worry about. Is that nonsense? Have words lost their meaning? If we reflect on those who have fought and suffered and died on the battlefield in the cause of their country and ours, can we rest satisfied with an acknowledgment that they have fulfilled their contractual obligations? And are we not bound to them by an invisible compact? Lincoln understood and stated the truth at Gettysburg. "In a larger sense we cannot dedicate—we cannot consecrate —we cannot hallow—this ground. The brave men, living and dead, who struggled here, have consecrated it far above our poor power to add or detract. . . . It is for us, the living, rather, to be dedicated here to the unfinished work which they who fought here have thus far so nobly advanced." If our nation is a moral essence we are bound to those who have made such sacrifices under the great primeval contract of eternal society to which we must bend our wills and our natures. Burke was stating a hard fact when he said that there is a partnership between those who are living, those who are dead, and those who are to be born. If there is no such partnership, if there is no mysterious incorporation of the human race, if there is no linking of one generation with another, men would become, as Burke said, "little better than the flies of a summer."

Man is therefore inescapably under the jurisdiction of the moral law, whether or not he is willing to acknowledge the fact. But a good society is possible only as its members feel an allegiance to principle. Burke knew better than most how difficult it is to apply the principle of law to a particular case, and what judgment, prudence, and wisdom may be necessary to avoid doing injustice even while guided by the principle of justice. He frequently maintained that he would never discuss the right or wrong of something until he knew all the circumstances, which give each situation its distinguishing characteristics. But Burke said that all law is only declaratory of eternal principles. He often stated that it is dangerous in the extreme to hold that law is merely the will of the state, and equally dangerous to believe that moral goodness is merely the inclination of the individual. Above us all, governors and governed, kings and subjects, there is the eternal moral law, which in jurisprudence from Cicero down to modern times has been called the Law of Nature.[2] In this theory of law Burke was deeply read. To it he made his final appeal whenever considerations of utility or prudence threatened to alter "the substance of original justice."

In his trial Warren Hastings pleaded that his brutalities in the government of India were necessary to control the people of that land, that India was not England,

that previous conquerors had been equally brutal, and
that he had authority granted him by the East India
Company and the government of England to take whatever steps were necessary in his judgment to subdue the
natives. Burke heaped some scorn on the idea of "geographical morality" and then continued: "Mr. Hastings comes before you. . . . He says, 'I had arbitrary
power to exercise, and I exercised it. Slaves I found
the people, slaves they are; they are so by their constitution; I did not make it for them; I was unfortunately
bound to exercise arbitrary power, and I did exercise
it.' In India, to use the words of Mr. Hastings, the
power of the sovereign was everything, the rights of
the people nothing. . . . He makes the corrupt practices of mankind the principles of his government; he
collects together the vicious examples of all the robbers
and plunderers of Asia, forms the mass of their abuses
into a code, and calls it the duty of a British governor.
. . . I believe so audacious a thing was never before
attempted by man. 'He had arbitrary power!' My
Lords, the East India Company have not arbitrary
power to give him. The king has no arbitrary power to
give. Neither your Lordships, nor the Commons, nor
the whole Legislature, have arbitrary power to give.
Arbitrary power is a thing which no man can give. My
Lords, no man can govern himself by his own will;
much less can he be governed by the will of others. We
are all born—high as well as low—governors as well
as governed—in subjection to one great, immutable,
pre-existing law, a law prior to all our devices and all

our conspiracies, paramount to our feelings, by which we are connected in the eternal frame of the universe, and out of which we cannot stir. This great law does not arise from our combinations and compacts; on the contrary, it gives them all the sanction they can have. Every good and perfect gift is of God; all power is of God; and He who has given the power, and from whom alone it originates, will never suffer it to be corrupted."

Thus the genius of Burke leads us back to the Law of Nature, the conscience of mankind, the rejection of which we observed in the first chapter. In his work we may find a searching critical examination of some fashionable speculations and doctrines. But the greatness of his constructive mind appears in his reinterpretation of the wisdom of the Ancients. Wordsworth, like Coleridge, had been for a time a disciple of Godwin. But in his *Prelude*, completed in 1805, only eight years after the death of Burke, he paid a tribute to the memory of the statesman which is both sympathetic and understanding:

> Genius of Burke! forgive the pen seduced
> By specious wonders, and too slow to tell
> Of what the ingenuous, what bewildered men,
> Beginning to mistrust their boastful guides,
> And wise men, willing to grow wiser, caught,
> Rapt auditors! from thy most eloquent tongue—
> Now mute, for ever mute in the cold grave.
> I see him,—old, but vigorous in age,—
> Stand like an oak whose stag-horn branches start
> Out of its leafy brow, the more to awe
> The younger brethren of the grove,

While he forewarns, denounces, launches forth
Against all systems built on abstract rights
Keen ridicule; the majesty proclaims
Of Institutes and Laws, hallowed by time;
Declares the vital power of social ties
Endeared by Custom; and with high disdain,
Exploding upstart Theory, insists
Upon the allegiance to which men are born.

# EPILOGUE: A MEDITATION ON THE SPIRIT OF MAN

There is a large element of truth in the dictum of Alexander Pope that the proper study of mankind is man. It is not only a proper study, but also natural and necessary. Our interests are inevitably homocentric. We have a special desire to know about the world as the complexity which affects our lives, and we desire to know ourselves because living is full of problems. So much Pope certainly had in mind. But in the more than two centuries since Pope, the efforts to explore the nature of man have given such a statement as his a meaning far more acute than it could have had for him. The history of these efforts provides an instructive subject for reflection and should indicate also how we should proceed in order to avoid pitfalls and to reach conclusions regarding the nature of man which conform in some degree to our experience. The history of thought since 1700 can be written in many ways, as the history of metaphysics, of logic, of political theory, of ethical theory, or of scientific discovery. But it can also be written as the history of theories of human nature, and to that central theme all these other modes of theoretical and practical intellection can be related. Such an orientation offers this great advantage to us ordinary laymen in philosophy, untrained as we are in the dialectic of the professional students, in that we can test and validate philosophical propositions by our own experience and our knowledge of the experience of mankind.

In the preceding pages an attempt has been made to present some episodes in this continuing search for the true philosophy of human nature. First, we noted that the Enlightenment rejected the juridical doctrine of the Law of Nature and all its assumptions and implications; next, the philosophers turned their search in another direction and elaborated substitute doctrines; finally, Burke rejected these substitutes and reaffirmed the ancient doctrine. Thus our narrative comes full circle. But history continued on, and, as has been indicated from time to time in the preceding account, the ideas contesting for supremacy in the eighteenth century have persisted in modified forms down to the present time. Specifically, we are to a marked degree the continuators of the Enlightenment in our persistent inclination to expect from science the final and complete explanation of our human nature and destiny.

A theory of human nature can be given by Divine Revelation, or be derived from some comprehensive philosophical or theological system, or be deduced from scientific generalizations, such as the theory of evolution. But some of the great truths are sufficiently available to the simple. A mere layman may look inwardly at his own experience, or outwardly, without too much erudition, at the experience of others recorded in history or presented to his own observation.

Indeed, it is quite the standard procedure in philosophical discussion to bring an abstract proposition down to the level of those concrete situations from which it might have been generated. Such reference of the general to the experienced particulars has always been practiced in philosophy, not only as a test of the general proposition, but also as a means of discovery.

Let us return to the theory of law and see how a simple everyday statement may bring with it a train of consequences not always at first expected. A man on the street might tell an inquiring reporter that he thinks law is the means whereby conflicting claims are settled by compromise and agreement, and that the ideal of law is this reconciliation of interests within a society. Such a statement would already constitute a considerable commitment to a theory of human behavior and of human society which, if not qualified, would lead to Utilitarianism. Suppose that on further interrogation the man can find nothing further to add, that he decides that he has said all that can profitably be said about the nature of law, then under a Socratic inquisition further implications would be discovered, and further theories would be generated regarding human nature, society, government, morals, and even metaphysics. The man would reveal a kind of Positivistic mentality. But let us approach this same man at another time, when he is embittered, as almost all men are at some time or other, over some results of this process of compromise and reconciliation of interests; he denounces them, not just

in personal anger, but with righteous indignation (one
of the most common of human emotions), and lo! he
has, wittingly or unwittingly, moved beyond both Utilitarianism and Positivism and demanded that the whole
theory of law be subject to considerations of another
kind and on another level. When a man in that state
of mind criticizes law or society, the idea of Justice is
born in him. He then commits himself to a whole new
series of propositions regarding man and society and
the universe. It has been well said that man is incurably
metaphysical. For even when we do not fully realize
it, we live by ideas which are a necessity to our being
but which we permit to remain in solution in our concrete experience.

It is therefore possible for us, even as laymen, to
draw a good deal of philosophy from our experience
and observation of human nature. It is remarkable
how durable human nature seems to be and how impossible it is to root out some of its aspirations. We
have been bombarded with many theories during the
last two centuries and we bear the scars, but we continue to live on essentially the same terms as our an-
cestors before the new theories were advanced. The
representation of human nature in the great literature
of the distant past continues to appear valid in our
modern experience. The sociologists may produce sta-
tistics to show that marriages endure on the average for
three years, or four years, or whatever the figure, but
no bride will permit the song to be changed to "Not for
a day, not for a year, but for three and one-half years."

The first rule in the book of the educational psychologists was for some time that a parent or teacher should never say "Don't" to a child; but the policing of school children at street crossings remains the standard practice. The remarkable success of school athletic programs, in which no one questions the necessity of old-fashioned rigorous training in fundamentals, contrasts sharply with the controversial results of the *laissez-faire* procedure so much favored in the classrooms. Communist ideology picked up the theory, advanced here and there by advanced thinkers down through the ages, that the family is an indefensible relic of the past and should be replaced by a more scientifically contrived arrangement; but Russian Communism learned long ago that this particular sacred doctrine of Engels had to be rejected; they even imposed a progressive tax on divorces to discourage them, and they have for some time been bringing up their children in such deference and respect for parents and elders as would not be tolerated by children in the United States. If such observations are considered thoughtfully, we can draw from them, not only knowledge about human nature, but some wisdom in dealing with it. All programs for the life of man must be adjusted to his real nature, of which, as Burke said, reason is but a part.

The spirit of man has been a stumbling block for all systematic philosophers of science. We may ponder the peculiar conclusions of the many distinguished apologists for science in the nineteenth century who attempted to reconcile human values to science by ex-

plaining them as natural developments out of the cosmic process and therefore really a part of it. But their
conclusions more commend their personal goodness
and nobility of character than their scientific acumen.
Their starting point was the latest great scientific discovery, the evolution of species. This offered some difficulty inasmuch as the Nature described by the science
of biology was, in Tennyson's phrase, "red in tooth and
claw," and all living things had to engage in a perilous
fierce struggle for existence. But the theory of evolution emphasized two fundamental biological goals in
this struggle, the survival of the individual, which had
often to be sacrificed, and the survival of the species,
which seemed to have priority. Biologists who desired
to base a "higher" morality on their own science usually looked with special benignity on the urge to per-
petuate the species. They were delighted with the observation that among the more complex and higher
forms of animal life the species could be perpetuated
only by maternal care of the newly born and sometimes
by the mutual aid in a society of adults. Herbert Spencer believed that such biological developments were
the origin and explanation of an ethics of benevolence
among the higher anthropoids and that our best traditional morality therefore has a solid foundation in
biology. Admittedly, there are conflicts between the
urge for individual survival and the urge for the survival of the species, but these may all be resolved when
the individual perceives how preferable long-range
beneficence is over short-term selfishness, when his

"lower" impulses yield to his "higher" impulses and he moves in the direction of that perfection of humanity which, unhappily, is still to be realized. But Spencer was an optimist regarding the future, for the biological urges are mighty and will prevail.

Another eminent philosopher of biology, Ernst Haeckel, sought to establish a human ethics on a broad investigation of the "duties of vertebrates." A vertebrate has duties to himself and to the fellow members of his species, and the balance between the two kinds of duties gives us, opined Haeckel, nothing less than the Golden Rule. Haeckel no doubt felt a genuine need for moral idealism and tried to justify it scientifically by his analysis of the struggle for existence. All this philosophy can be summed up in the sonorous and imaginative sentence of John Fiske: "The Earth spirit goes on, un-hasting yet unresting, weaving in the loom of Time the visible garment of God."

One may hesitate to accept this morality of the vertebrates, in the first place, because it exercises an arbitrary selectivity not authenticated by the cosmic process. The mother bear, who cares so assiduously for her cubs, is highly commended, whereas the male bear, who wants to kill and devour them, is ignored as philosophically insignificant. As a group, these scientific moralists were guilty of glossing over the brutalities of the struggle for existence. But there is also a more fundamental objection, that they were obliterating the distinction in meaning between "This is" and "This ought to be." It was after the time of Haeckel and Spen-

cer that Henri Poincaré warned that the language of
science is in the indicative, not in the imperative mood.
Thomas Huxley, also a distinguished spokesman for
science and the contemporary of Haeckel and Spencer,
declared that "of moral purpose I see no trace in Nature. That is an article of exclusively human manu-
facture—and very much to our credit." Human society, he insisted, must be considered distinct from
nature. "It is the more desirable, and even necessary,
to make this distinction, since society differs from nature in having a definite moral object; whence it comes
about that the course shaped by the ethical man—the
member of society or citizen—necessarily runs counter
to that which the non-ethical man—the primitive savage, or man as a mere member of the animal kingdom
—tends to adopt. The latter fights out the struggle for
existence to the bitter end, like any other animal; the
former devotes his best energies to the object of setting
limits to the struggle."

Huxley was probably not much interested in the implications of this break which he recognized between
the cosmic process and the spirit of man—if, indeed,
we could suppose him even to have been aware of them.
The important point is that this scientific observer observed the break and insisted on the reality of it. If we
try to understand quite objectively how such a being
as man came to exist on this planet, we encounter these
breaks—or perhaps they should be called "leaps," as
they are moments when something new seems to have
been added. At some point in time and space inert mat-

ter acquired life and the power of growth. At some later moment there occurred another leap and living beings with consciousness appeared. But for a philosophy of human nature these are not the major miracles of the cosmic process. Nor is it of major importance for us as human beings to learn that we and the whole universe in which we find ourselves are made up of such things as electrons and neutrons and protons, and that the physicist in his laboratory is really electrons studying electrons. Our kinship with Plato and Dante and Shakespeare and Beethoven remains unchanged. The "higher" vertebrates continue to have their "higher" duties. The spirit of man continues to disengage itself from the cosmic process, to rise above it, and to make demands upon it. It is the soul's discovery of itself that has established justice as an authoritative principle superior to revenge, raised love from an instinct to a spiritual power, acknowledged the imperative of the moral law, and awakened yearnings for realities of a transcendental kind. Man is *sui generis* in the cosmos, and the spirit of man can live only in an invisible world.

In order to understand human nature we must therefore begin by recognizing that, although man is a creature immersed in the cosmic process and the struggle for existence, he is unable to find mere continuing existence sufficient for his contentment. Man is incurably moral, incurably metaphysical, incurably religious. His greatest creations in art, music, and literature are full of anxiety and restlessness, full of his concern about the evil and the good. Dante said that his purpose in the *Paradiso* was to lead men from a state of wretchedness to a state of blessedness. It is in a struggle of that kind that the Spirit of Man has to contend, in a world of his ideals and aspirations, in which he may search with fear and trembling for his salvation. But darkness hangs over this world, as we know not only from great tragic drama but from life itself, and we sometimes see life saved and sometimes irretrievably lost. In our experience the good is as real as the evil, and the evil as real as the good. If there is a conceivable Heaven, it seems there must be a conceivable Hell. Such is the world into which we as human beings have been inducted and out of which we cannot stir. In the inscription over the gate of Dante's Inferno we read that Justice, Divine Power, Wisdom, and even Love had built the Abode of Damnation. Inversely, then, we may understand also that the existence of the Dolorous City bears testimony to the reality of the Justice, Power, Wisdom, and Love that built it.

> Giustizia mosse il mio alto Fattore;
> fecemi la divina Potestate,
> la somma Sapienza e il primo Amore.

# NOTES

## CHAPTER I

1. Werner Jaeger, *Paideia*, tr. by Gilbert Highet (Princeton, 1943), I, 181.
2. Aristotle *Rhetoric* I. xiii, xv.
3. Quotations from *De Legibus* are from the translation by C. W. Keyes in the Loeb Classical Library.
4. For a scholarly study of the importance of Natural Law in American judicature, see C. G. Haines, *The Revival of Natural Law Concepts* (1930).
5. Montaigne, *Essays* (Everyman edition), II, 297; I, 114; II, 301.
6. Brooks Adams, *Civilization and the Law* (1906), pp. 23, 45, 63–64.
7. Hobbes, *Leviathan*, Part I, chap. 11; Part II, chap. 26 and 21.
8. John Austin, *Lectures on Jurisprudence* (3rd ed.; 1869), p. 88.
9. A. P. d'Entrèves, *Natural Law* (1951), p. 110.
10. Lord Bryce, "The Law of Nature," in *Studies in History and Jurisprudence* (1901), Vol. II.

## CHAPTER II

1. John Donne, "The First Anniversary," ll. 205–14.
2. *Leviathan*, Part I, chap. iv.
3. *De Cive*, ed. Sterling P. Lamprecht (1949), p. 3.
4. Descartes, *The Method, Meditations, and Selections from the Principles*, tr. by John Veitch (6th ed.; 1879), p. 184.

5. Henri Gouhier, *La Pensée religieuse de Descartes* (1924), pp. 66–72, 142–48, and 150.

6. Leibnitz, *New Essays Concerning Human Understanding*, tr. by Alfred G. Langley (1896), p. 436.

7. Louis Couturat, *La Logique de Leibnitz* (1901), pp. 141, 84, note 3, and 98, note 3. Translation quoted from J. G. Hibben, *The Philosophy of the Enlightenment* (1910), p. 165.

8. Couturat, p. 240.

9. Pope, *The Dunciad*, Book IV, ll. 31, 647, and 462, and the article on Craig in *D.N.B.*

10. Hutcheson, *Inquiry* (2d ed.; 1726), pp. 182–84.

11. William R. Scott, *Francis Hutcheson* (1900), p. 32, note.

12. Fontenelle, *Preface sur l'utilité des mathématiques et de la physique*, in *Oeuvres* (1825), I, 54.

13. Locke, *Essay*, I, ii, 1; III, xi, 16; IV, iii, 18–19; IV, iv, 7–9; IV, xii, 8.

14. *Ibid.*, IV, viii.

15. *Ibid.*, II, i, 10–19.

16. *Ibid.*, IV, iii, 18.

17. John Wild, *George Berkeley* (1936), p. 29.

18. Helvetius, *A Treatise on Man*, tr. by W. Hooper (London, 1777), II, 447; also I, 202.

19. *Ibid.*, II, 422–23.

20. *Ibid.*, I, 223.

21. *Ibid.*, II, 299, 301.

CHAPTER III

1. Quoted by Radoslav A. Tsanoff, *The Moral Ideals of Our Civilization* (1942), p. 155.

2. *Leviathan*, Part I, chap. 15.

3. La Rochefoucauld, *Maxims*, tr. by Kenneth Pratt (1931), pp. 57, 59, 77, 89, 157, 233.

4. *The Cambridge Platonists,* ed. E. T. Campagnac (1901), pp. 3–5.

5. *Ibid.,* p. 284.

6. *Ibid.,* p. 70.

7. *Ibid.,* pp. 277–81.

8. *Ibid.,* pp. 68–69.

9. *Ibid.,* p. 46.

10. For the passages from the Anglican divines I am indebted to the article by Ronald S. Crane, "Suggestions toward a Genealogy of 'The Man of Feeling,' " in *ELH,* I (1934), 218–28.

11. *The Seasons, Spring,* 11. 349–51.

12. James Thomson, *Summer,* 11. 1379–84 and *Autumn,* 11. 669–72.

13. Joseph Warton, *The Enthusiast* (1744) and Thomas Warton, *The Pleasures of Melancholy* (1747).

14. *Characteristics,* ed. J. M. Robertson (1900), Vol. II, pp. 255, 265.

15. Mandeville, *Fable of the Bees,* ed. F. B. Kaye (1924), Vol. I, p. 323.

**CHAPTER IV**

1. Cicero *De Officiis* I. 4.

2. *De Legibus,* II, v. 13.

3. Lois Whitney, *Primitivism and the Idea of Progress* (1934), pp. 80–81.

4. Diderot, *Supplement to Bougainville's "Travels,"* tr. by Ralph H. Bowen in *Rameau's Nephew* (1956), p. 234.

5. Chauncey B. Tinker, *Nature's Simple Plan* (1922), pp. 90–111.

6. *Summer,* 1. 1566.

7. John Morley, *Diderot* (1914), Vol. II, pp. 17–18.

8. *Ibid.*, pp. 16–17.

9. Diderot expressed himself clearly in an undated letter
   probably written to Naegeon:
   Regardez-y de près et vous verrez que le mot *liberté*
   est un mot vuide de sens. Qu'il n'y a point et qu'il ne
   peut y avoir d'êtres libres. Que nous ne sommes que ce
   que convient à l'ordre général, à l'organisation, à
   l'éducation, et à la chaîne des événements. Voilà
   ce qui dispose de nous invinciblement; on ne con-
   noît non plus qu'un être agisse sans motifs, qu'un
   des bras d'une balance se meuve sans l'action d'un
   poids; et le motif nous est toujours extérieur, étranger,
   attaché ou par la nature ou par une cause quelconque
   qui n'est pas nous. . . . Mais s'il n'y a point de liberté,
   il n'y a point d'action qui mérite la louange ou le blâme.
   Il n'y a ni vice ni vertu. Rien dont il faille récompenser
   ou châtier. Qu'est-ce qui distingue donc les hommes?
   La bienfaisance et la malfaisance. Le malfaisant est un
   homme qu'il faut détruire, mais non punir. La bienfaisance est une bonne fortune et non une vertu. Mais
   quoique l'homme bien ou malfaisant ne soit pas libre,
   l'homme n'en est pas moins un être qu'on modifie. C'est
   par cette raison qu'il faut détruire le malfaisant sur une
   place publique. De là les bons effets de l'exemple, des
   discours, de l'éducation, du plaisir, de la douleur, des
   grandeurs, de la misère, etc., de là une sorte de philosophie pleine de considèration qui attache fortement
   aux bons, qui n'irrite non plus contre le méchant que
   contre un ouragan qui nous remplit les yeux de pous-
   sière. Il n'y a qu'une sorte de causes, à proprement
   parler, ce sont les causes physiques. Il n'y a qu'une sorte
   de nécessité; c'est la même pour tous les êtres, quelque
   distinction qu'il nous plaise d'établir entre eux, ou qui
   y soit réelement. Voilà ce qui me reconcilie avec le
   genre humain . . . Ne rien reprocher aux autres, ne se
   repentir de rien; voilà les premiers pas vers la sagesse.
   Ce qui est hors de là, est prejugé, fausse philosophie.

Diderot, *Correspondance inédite*, ed. André Babelon, (Paris, 1931), Vol. I, pp. 310–11.

**CHAPTER V**

*1.* J. B. Bury, *The Idea of Progress* (1920), pp. 221–22.
2. Helvetius, *A Treatise on Man*, I, 6–7.
*3. Ibid.*, II, 392–97.
*4. Ibid.*, II, 433, 435.
5. J. B. Bury, *The Idea of Progress*, pp. 241, 246.
6. Carl L. Becker, *The Heavenly City of the Eighteenth-Century Philosophers* (1932), pp. 150–51.
7. Compare the verdict on these philosophers by such a judicious scholar as Gustave Lanson:

> Tous ces faiseurs de systèmes posent des principes, donnent des définitions, et ils tirent des conséquences sans avoir songé à établir leurs principes ni à justifier leurs définitions. . . . Ils ne songent pas à se demander si la réalité autorise leurs principes ou leurs définitions: ils trouvent la réalité au terme de leur analyse; et s'ils ne la trouvent pas, ils la condamnent. Leur méthode n'est ni critique, ni historique, ni expérimentale: elle est purement analytique. La réalité est citée par eux pour être jugée par leur systèmes. Ils sont portés à prendre toutes les idées claires et distinctes pour des idées vraies; il leur parait impossible qu'un enchaînement nécessaire d'idées claires et distinctes ne représente pas en définitive la nature réelle, et, dans les domaines où s'exerce la liberté humaine, ne exprime pas la seule réalité légitime: en sorte que toute réalité qui n'y est pas conforme doit disparaître et faire place à une réalité conforme.

Gustave Lanson, *Études d'histoire littéraire* (1930), p. 91.

*8.* I. K. Luppol, *Diderot, ses idées philosophiques*, tr. par V. et Y. Feldman (1936), pp. 302–3.

9. William Godwin, *Enquiry Concerning Political Justice,*
   ed. F. E. L. Priestley, 3 vols. (1946), I, 124.
10. *Ibid.,* I, 88.
11. *Ibid.,* I, 89.
12. *Ibid.,* I, 92.
13. *Ibid.,* I, 433.
14. *Ibid.,* I, 126.
15. *Ibid.,* I, 126–29.
16. *Ibid.,* II, 453.
17. *Ibid.,* I, 135.
18. *Ibid.,* II, 464.
19. *Ibid.,* II, 210–11.
20. *Ibid.,* II, 211 and 528.

CHAPTER VI

1. F. J. C. Hearnshaw, *The Social and Political Ideas of
   Some Representative Thinkers of the Revolutionary Era*
   (1931), p. 93.
2. See Charles Parkin, *The Moral Basis of Burke's Political Thought* (1956), and Peter J. Stanlis, *Edmund
   Burke and the Natural Law* (1958).